The Gift-Giver's COOKBOOK

Judith Choate
Jane Green

Weidenfeld & Nicolson
New York

A WEIDENFELD & NICOLSON/FRIEDMAN GROUP BOOK

Copyright © 1989 by Michael Friedman Publishing Group, Inc.

Published in the United States by
Weidenfeld & Nicolson, New York
A Division of Wheatland Corporation
841 Broadway
New York, New York 10003-4793

Published in Canada by General Publishing Company, Ltd.

Library of Congress Cataloging-in-Publication Data

Choate, Judith.
    The gift-giver's cookbook / Judith Choate and Jane Green. — Rev.
ed., 1st ed.
        p.   cm.
    Includes index.
    ISBN 1-55584-322-0
    1. Baking   2. Confectionery.   3. Canning and preserving.
I. Green, Jane.   II. Title.
TX765.G8   1989
641.8--dc19   89-30863
                                                CIP

THE GIFT-GIVER'S COOKBOOK
was prepared and produced by
Michael Friedman Publishing Group
15 West 26th Street
New York, New York 10010

Art Director: Robert Kosturko
Designer: David Shultz
Photography Editor: Christopher Bain
Photo Researcher: Daniella Jo Nilva
Production Manager: Karen L. Greenberg

Typeset by BPE Graphics, Inc.
Color separations by Universal Colour Scanning, Ltd.
Printed and bound in Hong Kong by Leefung-Asco Printers, Ltd.

First Edition 1989

10 9 8 7 6 5 4 3 2 1

Dedication
For Dan

Revision Notes

In the almost twenty years that have passed since we wrote the first edition of *The Gift-Giver's Cookbook,* America's dining habits have changed considerably. International and regional foodstuffs are now commonplace in the supermarket and salad bars and health and fitness consciousness have become ingrained into the fast-food generation. In addition, the household cook more often than not has a demanding career and must use organizational skills to run a home smoothly. And yet, with these changes, a basic commitment to high-quality food has remained constant. And "homemade" is more welcome than ever!

In the first edition of *The Gift-Giver's Cookbook* we wanted to provide the home cook with flavorful, truly American kitchen alternatives to store-bought presents. We still do! Some of the recipes were ahead of their time and some were in the manner of the nineteenth century. Most of them remain in this revision—some with minor changes to accommodate our taste for less salt and less sugar and to allow for the inclusion of the now widely available regional American and international food products. We have added a small section devoted to low-calorie and special-diet recipes and have also indicated low-calorie recipes with a symbol (☆) throughout the book.

The sentiments we expressed in the first edition remain unchanged. With now-grown children and closely watched waistlines, we still find our friendship sealed in sharing the rewards of working in the kitchen. And now, our husbands even join us! We hope you will, too.

CONTENTS

Introduction

We think that there is nothing nicer to give or receive than a gift made in someone's kitchen, and we feel that most of our friends would agree. Particularly now that gift giving has become such a frenzied and commercialized activity, homemade gifts are unmistakably personal and convey to your friends and business associates that you have really given of yourself.

Throughout the year—and especially at holiday time while others are struggling with long shopping lists in overcrowded stores—you can remain in the warmth and friendliness of your own kitchen preparing gifts to please each recipient.

A well-stocked pantry or freezer of homemade food provides gifts for any occasion. Whenever we go to a party we present our hostess with something homemade: it can be a jar of jam or jelly, a fruit syrup or something as simple as salted or spiced nuts or an herbed rice. Whatever we choose is always welcomed! A bouquet of inexpensive kitchen gadgets and nonperishable homemade edibles is perfect for a housewarming or a wedding shower. Plastic toys packed with cookies or candy are great gifts for children. In fact, when any occasion calls for a gift, make it yourself!

We have found that it is not only a pleasure to receive homemade foods but even more delightful to make them. Working with a friend increases the fun, the yield, the recipes and provides a shoulder to cry on when the occasional kitchen disaster occurs. Your family can join in too: children love to make and decorate cutout cookies, and spouses can always be counted on to taste.

Homemade gifts cost very little. Our preparations start in midsummer when local fruits are ripe. Trips to the country yield wild berries and vegetables. In early August, peach orchards offer all you can pick, with immense savings over supermarket prices. And what a lovely way to spend the day! In early fall we all look forward to picking in the apple orchards. We have even enlisted friends and relatives across the country to send us their local nonperishable products—pecans from a Southern aunt, walnuts and dates from a brother in Southern California and fresh herbs from a friend's garden.

All through the year we save jars from instant coffee, baby food, mustard, mayonnaise, pickles, etc. They are the perfect sizes to hold homemade jams and jellies and eliminate the need to purchase jars made especially for this purpose. Coffee, nut, shortening and cookie tins, with your added decoration, make beautiful, personalized and cost-free containers for any confections. Fruit baskets (small ones like those in which Concord grapes, berries and cherry tomatoes are sold) also make marvelous gift containers when covered with aluminum foil or gift wrap and ribbon-tied.

In September, when the last batch of applesauce has been stored, we begin our Christmas baking with a fruitcake weekend. The first cakes are made from the recipes Judie's grandmother carried with her from Scotland in the early 1900's. She made her cakes in January and let them ripen all year long. Batches of light and dark fruitcakes are seasoned with brandy, wrapped and stored in a cool place, to make their first appearance on the Thanksgiving table along with the last one from the previous Christmas. Later on, we usually try a new recipe—a fruitcake richer, nuttier or more interesting than our usual one.

Recollections of Christmases past are filled with memories of holiday foods— the year the fruitcakes were especially good, the time our cookie-decorated tree was taken over by a colony of ants, the Gingerbread House whose roof kept shifting, the school-bus driver who started reminding us in June to be sure to remember his Christmas Date Bread, the Christmas Bubble Bread that kept rising until it pushed the oven door ajar. And all of them are filled with smells and tastes that make holidays truly memorable.

The recipes contained in this book are those we feel can be most easily made ahead of time, in fairly large quantities, stored or frozen and shipped without damage. Helpful information in each of these areas is included in the book. And always *label* your homemade gifts; people like to know what they are eating. We once received a thank-you from the recipient of a huge basket of homemade gifts that said, "We had no idea what we were eating, but it was all delicious." Since then, we have labeled each container of a homemade food.

There is almost no limit to the variety of gifts that you and your kitchen can produce. Not only the recipes in this book, but favorite casseroles, soups or salads that can be transported in plastic containers make wonderful gifts. We are sharing with you the rewards of many hours in our kitchens. We feel it is the nicest way of saying, "We're friends."

From the Oven

Carrot Cake

All Kinds of Cakes

© Steven Mark Needham/Envision

Almost all cake directions begin with the words "Cream butter and sugar until light and fluffy." This is one of the most important steps in successful cake making. If you use the butter at room temperature, it will be properly creamed with the sugar when the sugar has lost its graininess and the color is quite pale. If they are improperly creamed, the result will be a tough cake.

All of these cakes may be prepared in advance and frozen. Fruitcakes are most often seen on the Christmas table, but since they store well in a cool place and can be made in large quantities, they make excellent gifts all year round.

Most of the recipes list the necessary equipment. It is important to use the same measuring utensils for each ingredient, as there is often a difference in sets of measuring cups and spoons. Also, a rubber spatula and wire cooling racks will make cake baking easier. If you follow the instructions as given, you should have no trouble presenting your family or friends with a delicious and attractive cake.

Fruitcakes taste best and are least expensive when the chopped fruit is purchased in bulk. If you don't have a store specializing in dried fruits in your locale and you want to produce especially delicious cakes, we suggest that you order the fruits from one of the many mail-order gourmet catalogues available. You can, of course, buy chopped fruit in jars, but the end result will be both costlier and drier.

On the other hand, we suggest that you use spices freshly ground, as their flavor seems to hold up better through a long storage period.

A small pan of water placed on the bottom of the oven during the baking time will also produce a moister cake.

When freezing cakes, wrap them carefully in freezer wrap, label them and mark the date of baking. It is best not to freeze a cake for longer than three months. If you wish to frost or glaze the cake, this can be done either before or after freezing. Thaw a frozen cake at least one hour at room temperature before serving time.

There are two methods of preparing pans for the baking and storage of fruitcakes. You may line the pans either with greased heavy brown paper or with aluminum foil. If you use brown paper, you must remove it before wrapping the cake in a brandy-soaked cheesecloth for storage. If you use aluminum foil, it can be left on the cake as a storage wrapping. With the latter method, generously sprinkle brandy on the cake—individual taste will determine the amount. Either method requires airtight storage. An excellent container is a large plastic bag (such as those sold as garbage-can liners) sealed tightly.

Fruitcakes can, of course, be eaten immediately, but everyone knows that conventional fruitcakes improve with aging. What this means is periodically unsealing the airtight wrapping, sprinkling the cakes with brandy and resealing them. This can be done every two or three weeks, depending on how strong a brandy flavor you want.

Note that fruitcakes are not generally frozen, since they keep for long periods without freezing.

Plastic wrap, foil and disposable aluminum pans and paper goods make packaging and transporting gift cakes relatively simple.

© Steven Mark Needham/Envision

Chocolate Mousse Cake

Preheat oven to: 350 degrees
Utensils needed: Double boiler; Electric mixer; 1 9-inch spring-form pan, greased heavily and dusted with cocoa powder
Baking time: Approximately 30 minutes

¾ pound unsweetened chocolate	8 large egg yolks
1½ cup unsalted butter	1¾ cups superfine sugar
1 teaspoon instant espresso powder	2 tablespoons Kahlua
	8 large egg whites
	cocoa powder for dusting

Melt together the chocolate and butter in the top half of a double boiler over hot water, stirring constantly. When melted and well blended, stir in espresso powder and remove from heat. Set aside.

Beat the egg yolks until very light. Gradually add sugar, beating constantly. Beat until mixture falls in ribbons off the beaters. Stir in Kahlua. Set aside.

Beat the egg whites until stiff but not dry. Set aside.

Slowly whisk the chocolate into the egg yolk mixture until well blended. Stir in ½ of the beaten egg whites until well blended. Softly but thoroughly whisk in remaining egg whites.

Pour into prepared pan reserving 1 cup batter. Bake at 350 degrees for approximately 30 minutes or until center is set (the top might be cracked). Cool in pan on wire rack.

Remove cooled cake from pan and place on service (or storage) dish. Spread remaining chocolate mixture on top and dust with cocoa. Cover loosely and refrigerate for at least 6 hours before serving time.

Judie's Rich Chocolate-Chunk Cake

Preheat oven to: 350 degrees
Utensils needed: Electric mixer; 1 9-inch spring-form tube pan, greased and floured
Baking time: Approximately 45 minutes

1 cup condensed milk	1 cup milk
2 squares unsweetened chocolate	2 cups sifted all-purpose flour
½ cup unsalted butter	½ cup cocoa powder, sifted
1½ cups sugar	1 teaspoon pure vanilla extract
2 eggs	½ cup semisweet chocolate chunks
1 teaspoon baking soda	

Place condensed milk and chocolate squares in heavy saucepan over medium heat. Bring to boil; stir until mixture reaches pudding consistency. Remove from heat. Cool.

Cream butter and sugar until light and fluffy. Add eggs and beat into mixture. When well blended, add chocolate mixture. Stir the baking soda into the milk. Add to batter. Sift the flour and cocoa into the batter and mix well. Stir in the vanilla. Fold in the chocolate chunks, making sure that they are evenly distributed through the batter.

Pour into prepared pan. Bake at 350 degrees for about 45 minutes or until edges pull away from sides of pan. Cool slightly in pan. Remove the cake and finish cooling on wire rack. Serve at room temperature.

Apricot-Brandy Pound Cake

Preheat oven to: 325 degrees
Utensils needed: Electric mixer; 3-quart bundt pan, greased and floured
Baking time: 1¼ hours

1 cup softened unsalted butter	3 cups sifted cake flour
2½ cups sugar	¼ teaspoon baking soda
6 large eggs	1 cup sour cream
1½ teaspoons pure vanilla extract	½ cup apricot brandy
1½ teaspoons orange extract	

Cream butter and sugar together until light and fluffy. Add eggs one at a time, beating well after each addition. Add vanilla and orange extracts.

© Steven Mark Needham/Envision

Sift together flour and baking soda. Add alternately to butter-sugar mixture with the sour cream and brandy. Mix well.

Pour batter into prepared pan and bake at 325 degrees for 1¼ hours or until edges pull away from sides of pan. Cool in pan for 15 minutes before removing cake. Continue cooling on wire rack.

Bundt Cake

Preheat oven to: 350 degrees
Utensils needed: Electric mixer; 3-quart bundt pan, greased and floured
Baking time: 30 to 40 minutes

1 cup unsalted butter	1 cup milk
2 cups sugar	1 teaspoon pure vanilla extract
3 cups sifted all-purpose flour	2 teaspoons baking powder
4 large eggs	

Cream together the butter and sugar until light and fluffy. Add the flour a little bit at a time with one egg and ¼ cup milk. Beat well. Continue adding flour and eggs and milk until all are beaten in. Blend in the vanilla and baking powder. Mix well.

Pour into prepared pan. Bake at 350 degrees for 30 to 40 minutes or until edges pull away from sides of pan. Remove from pan and cool on wire rack.

VARIATIONS:
1. Mix in one cup finely chopped nuts.
2. Marbleize cake by loosely stirring in ¼ cup cocoa.

Macadamia-Nut Cake

Preheat oven to: 350 degrees
Utensils needed: Electric mixer; 3 8-inch loaf
pans, greased and floured
Baking time: 45 minutes

1 cup unsalted butter
1 cup white sugar
¾ cup loosely packed
light-brown sugar
4 large eggs
2 teaspoons pure
vanilla extract
3 cups sifted cake
flour

1 tablespoon baking
powder
2 tablespoons cocoa
powder
1 cup half-and-half
2½ cups chopped
macadamia nuts

Cream the butter and both sugars until light and
fluffy. Add the eggs and vanilla and beat until well
blended. Sift together the cake flour, baking powder and cocoa. Add the sifted dry ingredients
alternately with the half-and-half to the creamed
mixture. Beat until well mixed. Stir in nuts. Pour
equal portions of batter into prepared pans and
bake at 350 degrees for 45 minutes or until edges
pull away from pans.

Cool in pans for 15 minutes. Then remove from
pans and cool on wire rack.

Orange Pound Cake

Preheat oven to: 350 degrees
Utensils needed: Electric mixer; 1 10-inch
tube pan, greased and floured
Baking time: 40 to 50 minutes

¾ cup unsalted
butter
1½ cups sugar
2 large eggs
1 teaspoon pure
vanilla extract
2 cups sifted all-
purpose flour
1 teaspoon baking
soda

1 cup sour cream
1½ teaspoons grated
fresh orange rind

TOPPING
½ cup sugar
½ cup orange juice
4 tablespoons orange
liqueur (optional)

© L & M Photo/FPG International

Cream the butter and sugar together until light and
fluffy. Add the eggs one at a time, beating well after
each addition. Add the vanilla.

Sift together the flour and baking soda. Gradually add the sifted dry ingredients to the butter-
sugar mixture alternately with the sour cream. Beat
well. Add the orange rind and mix well.

Pour into prepared pan. Bake at 350 degrees for
40 to 50 minutes, or until edges pull away from
sides of pan. Remove cake from oven.

Boil together sugar and orange juice for topping
until sugar is dissolved. Add orange liqueur if desired. While cake is still hot, pour this mixture over
the top. When cake is cold, remove from pan.

© Steven Mark Needham/Envision

Cream butter thoroughly. Add sugar gradually, creaming with butter until mixture is very light and fluffy. Add eggs one at a time, beating well after each addition. Gradually stir in flour, blending until smooth. Stir in walnuts and vanilla and mix well. Pour into 3 prepared 9-inch loaf pans.

Bake at 325 degrees for 1 hour or until cake is springy to touch and toothpick inserted in the middle comes out clean. Remove from pan and cool on wire rack.

VARIATIONS:

1. For 1 of the 2 cups of finely chopped walnuts, substitute 1 cup chocolate bits (or other flavored bits).

2. Add to the basic mixture 1 teaspoon cinnamon and 2 teaspoons grated fresh orange or lemon rind.

3. Substitute 2 tablespoons liqueur or brandy for the 1 tablespoon vanilla extract.

Jane's Walnut Pound Cake

Preheat oven to: 325 degrees
Utensils needed: Electric mixer; 3 9-inch loaf pans, lined with waxed paper, buttered or floured
Baking time: 1 hour

1 pound unsalted butter	2 cups finely chopped walnuts
2 cups sugar	1 tablespoon pure vanilla extract
10 large eggs	
4 cups sifted cake flour	

Carrot Cake

Preheat oven to: 350 degrees
Utensils needed: Electric mixer; 1 9-inch bundt pan, greased and floured, or 2 9-inch round cake pans, greased and floured
Baking time: Approximately 60 minutes for tube pan; 35 minutes for round pans

4 large eggs	1½ teaspoon baking soda
1 cup vegetable oil	2 teaspoons ground cinnamon
½ cup buttermilk	¼ teaspoon ground cloves
¾ cup white sugar	dash ground ginger
½ cup light-brown sugar	
2 cups all-purpose flour	

2 teaspoons pure
  vanilla extract
2 cups grated fresh
  carrots

1 cup chopped black
  walnuts (any nut
  may be substituted)
Cream-Cheese
  Frosting (optional)

NOTE: This frosting freezes and thaws particularly well and can be used on most any cake calling for a sweet frosting.

Beat the eggs until well blended. Add oil, buttermilk and sugars and beat until smooth. Sift together the flour, baking soda and spices and add to egg mixture. When well blended, stir in vanilla, carrots and walnuts.

Pour into prepared pan(s). Bake at 350 degrees for approximately 60 minutes for bundt pan or 35 minutes for 9-inch round cake pans or until a wooden toothpick placed in the center comes out clean. Remove from pan and cool on wire rack. When cool, frost with Cream-Cheese Frosting, if desired.

Cream-Cheese Frosting

Utensils needed: Electric mixer

1 cup softened
  cream cheese
½ cup softened
  unsalted butter
1 teaspoon pure
  vanilla extract
1 teaspoon grated
  fresh lemon rind

1 teaspoon fresh
  orange juice
2½ cups
  confectioner's
  sugar

Beat the cream cheese and butter until light and fluffy. Add remaining ingredients and beat until smooth.

Filled Sour-Cream Cake

Preheat oven to: 375 degrees
Utensils needed: Electric mixer; 1 9-inch-square baking pan, greased and floured
Baking time: 40 minutes

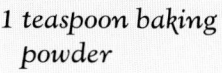

2 cups sifted all-
  purpose flour
1 teaspoon baking
  powder
1 teaspoon baking
  soda
1 cup unsalted butter
1 cup sugar
2 large eggs
1 cup sour cream

FILLING
1 cup chopped nuts
¼ cup firmly packed
  brown sugar
2 teaspoons ground
  cinnamon

Sift together the flour, baking powder and baking soda. In a separate bowl, cream together the butter and sugar until light and fluffy. Add eggs, beating thoroughly after each addition.

Into the creamed butter-sugar-egg mixture, blend the sifted dry ingredients alternately with the sour cream.

Pour half of the batter into prepared pan.

Mix the filling and sprinkle half on the batter. Pour in remaining batter and sprinkle remaining nut mixture over the top.

Bake at 375 degrees for about 40 minutes or until edges pull away from sides of pan. Remove from pan and cool on wire rack.

Our Favorite Cheesecake

Preheat oven to: 350 degrees
Utensils needed: Electric mixer; 1 9-inch
  spring-form pan, greased and floured,
  coated with extra-fine bread or graham
  cracker crumbs
Baking time: Approximately 1 hour

2 pounds cream cheese	vanilla extract
1 cup sugar	1 teaspoon grated fresh lemon rind
5 large eggs	Sour-Cream Topping
2 teaspoons pure	(optional)

Cream sugar and cream cheese until very smooth. Add eggs, one at a time, beating well after each addition. Stir in vanilla and lemon rind.

Pour into prepared pan. Bake at 350 degrees for approximately 1 hour or until center is firm. (Do not turn off oven if using Sour-Cream Topping.) Let stand for 15 minutes before topping.

Spread Sour-Cream Topping over top of cake. Return to 350-degree oven for 10 minutes. Remove from oven and cool on wire rack. Do not remove from pan until cake is well cooled.

Sour-Cream Topping

1½ cups sour cream	superfine sugar
2 tablespoons	1 teaspoon pure vanilla extract

Beat all ingredients together for about 3 minutes or until well blended. Spread over top of slightly cooled cheesecake as directed.

VARIATIONS:

1. For Marbleized Cheesecake: Stir 3 squares melted unsweetened chocolate into half of the cheesecake batter. Pour one-half of the remaining cheesecake batter into prepared pan and use a spatula to streak and swirl one-half of the chocolate batter through it. Repeat with remaining batters.

2. For Praline Cheesecake: Replace white sugar with light-brown sugar and add 1½ cups finely chopped pecans.

3. For Peanut Butter Cheesecake: Use 1½ pounds cream cheese and ¾ cup chunky peanut butter and add 1 cup semisweet chocolate bits.

© Steven Mark Needham/Envision

Gramma's Dark Fruitcake

Preheat oven to: 300 degrees
Utensils needed: Electric mixer; 10 6-inch loaf

pans, foil-lined
Baking time: 2 hours

1½ cups soft unsalted butter	1 pound white seedless raisins
1½ cups sugar	1 pound dark seedless raisins
8 large egg yolks	
⅔ cup white corn syrup	2 pounds chopped glazed fruit
1 teaspoon baking soda	1½ pounds whole pitted dates
1 cup sour milk	½ pound green glazed cherries
½ cup brandy (or fruit juice)	½ pound red glazed cherries
1 teaspoon orange extract	½ pound chopped glazed citron
2 tablespoons freshly ground cinnamon or 3 tablespoons canned ground cinnamon	¼ pound chopped glazed pineapple
	flour to make soft batter, about 7 cups
1½ cups sifted all-purpose flour	8 large egg whites
2 cups walnut pieces	¼ teaspoon cream of tartar
1½ pounds currants	

Cream the butter and sugar until light and fluffy. Add egg yolks and corn syrup and beat well. Stir baking soda into the sour milk and add to the creamed mixture. Continue mixing while you add the brandy, orange extract and cinnamon. Set aside.

In another bowl, place the nuts and fruits. Dredge them well with 1½ cups flour. Add the dredged fruits and nuts to the creamed mixture along with enough flour to make a soft batter. This must be mixed with your hands so that it will be easy to tell when a soft batter has been achieved. You will probably use about 7 cups of flour.

Add the cream of tartar to the egg whites in the large bowl of an electric mixer. Beat until stiff. Using your hands, lightly fold the stiff egg whites into the batter. Spoon batter into prepared pans, filling each about two-thirds full. Place a container of water in the bottom of the oven to prevent cakes from drying out.

Bake about 2 hours at 300 degrees or until edges pull away from the sides of the pans. Remove from pans and cool on wire racks.

Fresh Apple Cake

Preheat oven to: 350 degrees
Utensils needed: Electric mixer; 1 10-inch bundt pan, greased and floured
Baking time: 1 hour

2 large eggs	1 teaspoon ground cinnamon
1½ cups sugar	
1 cup vegetable oil	2½ cups peeled, cored and chopped fresh tart apples
2 teaspoons pure vanilla extract	
2½ cups all-purpose flour	1 cup chopped walnuts
1 teaspoon baking soda	1 cup yellow seedless raisins (optional)

Beat eggs and sugar together until well blended. Stir in oil and vanilla and beat until creamy. Sift dry ingredients together and blend into the creamed mixture. When well blended, stir in apples and walnuts (and raisins, if desired). Pour into prepared bundt pan.

Bake at 350 degrees for 1 hour or until edges pull away from sides of pan. Cool in pan or wire rack.

Super Chocolate Chess Cake

Preheat oven to: 350 degrees
Utensils needed: Electric mixer; 1 9-inch cake
    pan
Baking time: Approximately 35 minutes

½ cup unsalted
    butter
2 large egg yolks
1 large egg
3 tablespoons water
1 teaspoon white
    vinegar
1 cup sugar
½ cup cocoa powder

1 tablespoon all-
    purpose flour

Melt butter in a small pan over very low heat. Set aside but keep warm.

Beat egg yolks and egg until very well blended. Add water and vinegar and beat on high speed until frothy. On low speed, pour in melted butter and blend well. Mix sugar, flour and cocoa and slowly add to egg mixture. Beat until thoroughly blended.

Pour into prepared pan and bake at 350 degrees for approximately 35 minutes or until edges pull away from sides of pan and center is firm.

NOTE: This extraordinarily rich cake can be served frozen or at room temperature with a dollop of whipped cream.

Honey Cake

Preheat oven to: 350 degrees
Utensils needed: Electric mixer; 1 8-inch-
    square loaf pan, greased and floured
Baking time: About 45 minutes

½ cup unsalted
    butter
1 cup sugar
1 extra-large egg
2 cups sifted all-
    purpose flour
1 teaspoon baking
    soda
½ teaspoon ground
    cloves
½ teaspoon ground
    mace

1½ teaspoons ground
    cinnamon
1 cup sour milk
⅓ cup chopped nuts

TOPPING
2 tablespoons
    softened unsalted
    butter
4 tablespoons honey
2 tablespoons heavy
    cream
1 cup chopped nuts

Cream the butter and sugar until light and fluffy. Add the egg and blend well. Place the sifted flour, soda and spices in a sifter. Sift the dry ingredients alternately with the sour milk into the creamed mixture. Mix well. Stir in chopped nuts.

Pour into prepared pan and bake at 350 degrees for about 45 minutes or until edges pull away from sides of pan.

While cake is baking, prepare the topping. Blend the butter, honey, cream and nuts until well mixed. Spread the topping on the cake as soon as it is done. Place cake under broiler until topping browns slightly. Cool in pan on wire rack.

Gingerbread House

The joy and beauty of a Gingerbread House more than compensate for the amount of work involved in making one. Once you have created a house, you will want to make one every holiday season. To children, a Gingerbread House is a fairy tale come true, and to adults it is remembrances of Christmases long past.

The following steps will greatly aid you in planning and executing a successful Gingerbread House. Steps 2 and 5 can be family projects, while the other steps are best done by one person.

1. Using heavy cardboard, draw the pattern pieces for the house (see page 21). Be sure you measure carefully. Cut pieces with a sharp knife, labeling each as you go. Place all pattern pieces in a secure place.

2. Purchase the candy, cookies and nonedible decorations you will need.

3. Allow three days for the making of the house. On the first day, make the dough, cut it to the pattern and bake it. All pieces should be handled very carefully and stored in a safe place.

4. On the second day, "glue" the house together. If you are going to display it on a tray, glue the house to it.

5. On the third day, decorate your house. And enjoy it!

Preheat oven to: 350 degrees
Utensils needed: Electric mixer; At least 3 rimless cookie sheets, greased
Baking time: Approximately 12 to 15 minutes for large pieces, 5 to 7 minutes for small pieces.

The following recipe must be made twice for a complete house. You will have enough dough left for Gingerbread Men or cookie decorations for the house.

1 cup softened unsalted butter	2 teaspoons ground cinnamon
1 cup light-brown sugar	1 teaspoon ground nutmeg
½ cup molasses	1 teaspoon ground ginger
½ cup dark corn syrup	½ teaspoon ground mace
1 tablespoon grated fresh lemon rind	
6 cups sifted all-purpose flour	

Place the butter, brown sugar, molasses and corn syrup in a heavy saucepan over medium heat. Stir until all ingredients are melted. Keep warm.

Place the lemon rind in a large mixing bowl and resift the flour together with all other dry ingredients into the bowl.

Stir butter-syrup mixture into dry ingredients. Use your hands to combine, and knead thoroughly to incorporate the flour. This should produce a warm, firm mass of dough.

Place a large handful of dough on a greased rimless cookie sheet. Roll out to ⅛-inch thickness.

Dust cardboard pattern pieces lightly with flour. Place on dough and cut around them with a sharp knife. Remove leftover dough and save for further use. On wall pieces, cut out the windows with a small paring knife, and if you wish to make panes, form tiny strips of dough and fit into place.

When dough pieces are complete, chill for ½ hour before baking. Then bake in 350-degree oven for prescribed time or until firm and slightly browned at edges. Check from time to time during baking. If bubbles form, pat them down with a spatula, being careful not to tear dough.

Cool on pans until each piece is quite firm. Finish cooling on wire rack. Store securely until you are ready to build house.

TO ASSEMBLE HOUSE:

Melt 2 cups granulated sugar in a heavy skillet at least 12 inches across. Use very low heat to keep sugar from burning, and stir constantly until sugar is melted.

Starting with the walls, dip edges of the gingerbread pieces into the sugar-syrup glue. Work slowly. Make sure pieces are firmly stuck before adding on a new piece.

When the four walls are secure, dip a brush into the syrup glue and coat the tray on which you are going to place the house. Immediately set the frame on the prepared tray.

To place roof on house, dip inside edges, excluding the top edge, of one roof piece into syrup glue. Brush glue also on the slanting edges of end walls. Quickly set that half of roof in place, carefully lining up top edge with peak of side wall and leaving about ¾-inch overhang at each side edge. Make sure first half of roof is secure before gluing on the other half.

Drip glue along the top meeting edges of roof, and set the chimney piece about 2 inches in from one end in the crack formed by the meeting of the roof pieces.

Glue the door piece to one side of doorway, leaving it about half open.

To permit the glue to harden thoroughly, let the house sit undisturbed at least 24 hours before proceeding with the decoration.

You may also use Snow Icing to glue the house together but the seams will be more evident.

Snow Icing

1 pound
 confectioner's
 sugar, sifted
3 large egg whites,
 slightly beaten

1 teaspoon cream of
 tartar
drop of white vinegar

Prepare one batch of Snow Icing at a time. You will probably need at least two batches to complete the decoration.

Place sugar in small bowl of electric mixer. Add the slightly beaten egg whites, and beat together on lowest speed of mixer for about 1 minute.

Add cream of tartar and drop of vinegar and beat on high speed of electric mixer until icing is stiff and shiny, as for meringue.

TO DECORATE HOUSE

Spread Snow Icing liberally on the roof. Then immediately start setting candy or cookie trim in place on it. Any wafer-type cookies or nonpareils make excellent roof tiles.

With a finger, spread about ⅛ inch of icing around the window edges. Immediately decorate with small candy pieces to simulate shutters or paint trim.

Decorate the door and sides of house as you wish with icing.

Cover the tray with Snow Icing and place any desired "lawn" decoration in the icing. These can be small plastic items of the dimestore variety or more candy or gingerbread-cookie trim.

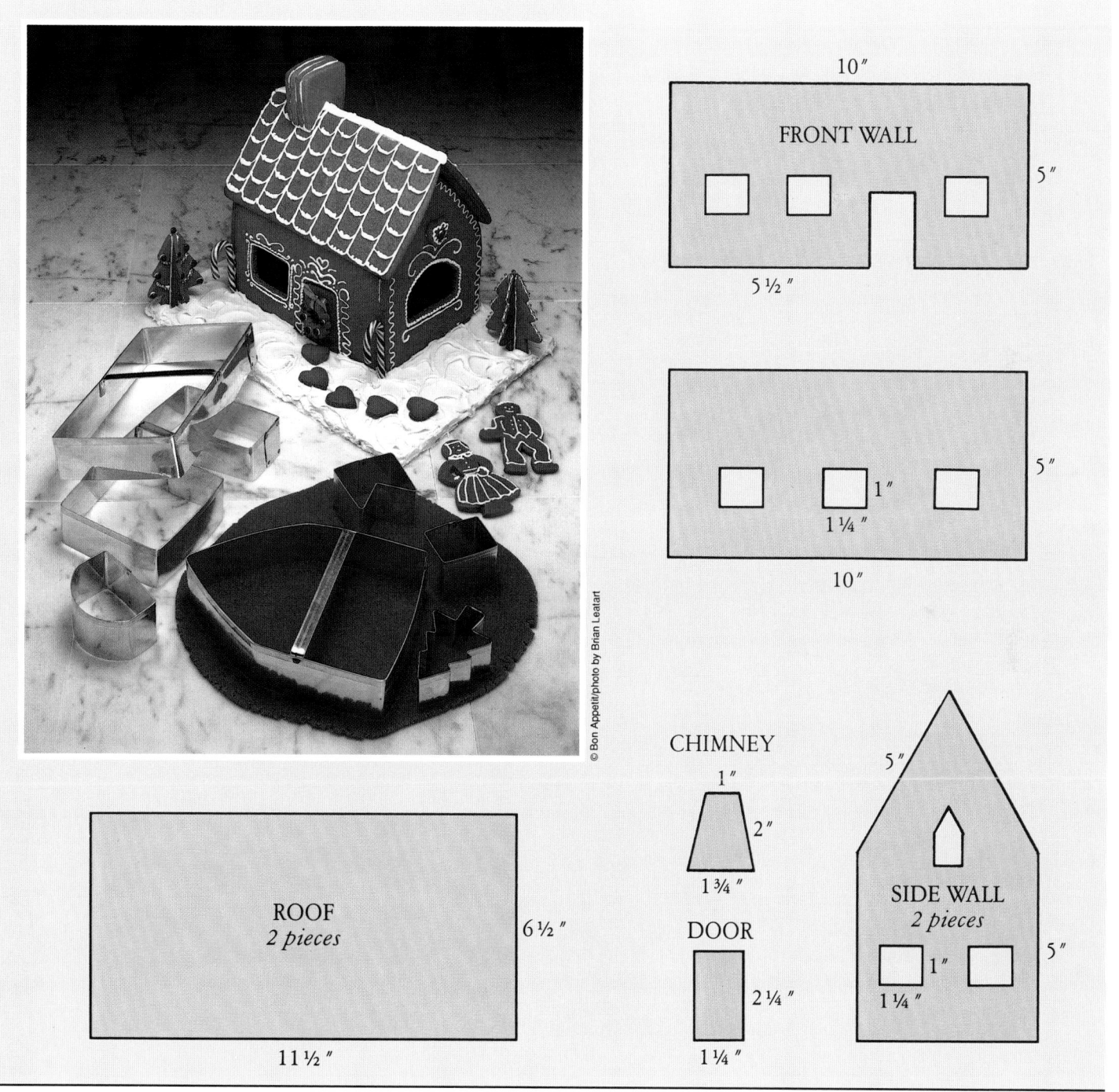

© Bon Appetit/photo by Brian Leatart

10"

FRONT WALL

5"

5 ½ "

5"

1"

1 ¼ "

10"

CHIMNEY

1"

2"

1 ¾ "

DOOR

2 ¼ "

1 ¼ "

5"

SIDE WALL
2 pieces

5"

1"

1 ¼ "

ROOF
2 pieces

6 ½ "

11 ½ "

All Kinds of Cakes

$\mathcal{B}$reads

Homemade bread is about the most unexpected treat that you can make for your family or friends. A gift of freshly made bread and a tub of homemade butter is something almost anyone will appreciate.

Most of the breads that we have chosen are "quick" breads—that is, breads made without yeast and quicker and easier to prepare than yeast breads. Quick loaf breads are especially nice made in small (6 x 3-inch) loaf pans which can be ordered from a gourmet store or a mail-order catalogue.

The yeast breads included are simple to make. If you have never made a yeast bread, your first loaf may be a disaster, but your next may be perfect. One of the most common errors in making yeast breads is dissolving the yeast in water either too hot or too cold. Use very warm water (105 to 115 degrees) for dry yeast, or lukewarm water (85 degrees) for compressed yeast. All other ingredients, unless otherwise specified, should be at room temperature. All breads in this chapter are easily frozen and will keep, wrapped airtight in freezer wrap, for up to three months.

Breads may be wrapped for gift giving in much the same way as loaf cakes. They are especially attractive wrapped airtight in plastic wrap, then covered with colored cellophane.

You may also wish to give them in a plastic bread-storage container which can be purchased in housewares departments of most large stores.

Yeast Breads

Spicy Salt Sticks

Preheat oven to: 400 degrees
Utensils needed: Electric mixer; 2 greased
* cookie sheets, salted and seeded*
Baking time: 15 to 20 minutes
Quantity: 2 dozen breadsticks
Storing: These keep for a long time. Use an
* empty cereal box or plastic container, and*
* place carefully so sticks remain unbroken*

1 package dry yeast
1¼ cups very warm
  water
3 tablespoons sugar
Tabasco sauce; to
  taste
4½ teaspoons
  caraway seed

1 tablespoon
  unsalted butter
¼ teaspoon onion
  powder
3½ cups sifted flour
2 tablespoons coarse
  salt

Dissolve yeast in 1¼ cups very warm water. Stir in sugar, Tabasco, 2½ teaspoons caraway seed, butter and onion powder. Sift in flour and mix well. Place dough on lightly floured board and knead until smooth and elastic, about 10 minutes. Turn into greased bowl, turn dough once, cover and let rise in warm place until double in bulk, about 1 hour.

Punch dough down, place on floured board and divide in half. Roll each half into a rectangle 12 inches long. Then cut each half into 12 equal strips. Roll each strip with hands into a rope 12 inches long by ⅓ inch thick.

Place 1 teaspoon caraway seed and 1 tablespoon coarse salt on each greased cookie sheet. Roll each rope piece in caraway-salt mixture. Place dough sticks on cookie sheet. Cover and let rise 1 hour or until double in bulk.

Bake at 400 degrees for 15 to 20 minutes or until lightly browned. Cool out of pan on wire racks. Handle carefully while warm.

Quick White Bread

Preheat oven to: 425 degrees
Utensils needed: Electric mixer with dough
* hook; 4 9-inch loaf pans, greased and*
* floured*
Baking time: 15 minutes at 425 degrees; 30
* minutes at 375 degrees*

2 cups milk
5 tablespoons sugar
2 tablespoons salt
  (optional or to
  taste)
2 packages yeast
Approximately 12
  cups sifted all-
  purpose flour

2 cups lukewarm
  water
2 tablespoons
  softened unsalted
  butter
5 tablespoons melted
  unsalted butter or
  vegetable
  shortening

Scald together the milk, sugar and salt; cool to lukewarm.

Dissolve yeast in 2 cups lukewarm water; add the lukewarm milk mixture. Stir in 6 cups flour and beat until smooth. Add melted butter and enough additional flour to produce an easily handled dough.

Knead dough quickly and lightly until smooth and elastic. Place dough in greased bowl, cover and let rise in a warm place for 1½ hours.

When dough has risen, divide into 4 equal portions and shape into loaves. Place loaves in prepared pans, cover and let rise until double in bulk, about 1 hour.

Bake at 425 degrees for 15 minutes; then reduce heat to 375 degrees and finish baking, about 30 minutes. While loaves are still hot, rub tops with softened butter. Cool on wire racks after removing from pans.

VARIATIONS:

1. For Raisin Bread: You may increase sugar to ½ cup, beat in 2 large eggs and 1 tablespoon ground cinnamon and knead in 2 cups of raisins.

2. For Wheat Bread: Add ⅓ cup molasses to milk mixture, decrease white flour to 4 cups, add 6 cups whole-wheat flour and 2 cups unsweetened wheat germ.

☆ French Bread

Preheat oven to: 375 degrees
Utensils needed: Electric mixer with dough hook; 2 clean damp cloths, plus glasses to hold them as cloth tents over rising bread; 2 greased cookie sheets, sprinkled with cornmeal

Baking time: 40 minutes
Quantity: 2 loaves

2 packages yeast	5½ cups sifted all-purpose flour
2½ cups lukewarm water	1 tablespoon water
2 cups sifted all-purpose flour	1 egg white, slightly beaten
1 tablespoon salt (optional)	

Mix the yeast into ½ cup lukewarm water.

In another bowl, sift together the flour and salt. Stir in the remaining 2 cups lukewarm water. Blend well. Add the dissolved yeast mixture. Blend together well. Stir in 4½ cups sifted flour. Cover tightly and let set for 10 minutes.

Then knead dough for 10 minutes, working in the remaining 1 cup sifted flour. Cover and let rise 1½ hours in a greased bowl set in a warm place.

Punch down dough and then let rise again for 1 hour as above. Divide dough into two parts. Cover each half with a deep bowl and let set again for 10 minutes.

Roll each half of dough as for a jelly roll. Starting at the narrow edge, tightly roll the dough into a French Bread shape.

Place each loaf on a prepared cookie sheet. With a sharp knife, make three slashes across the top of the loaf. Brush with egg white slightly beaten with water. Make a tent of a damp cloth, held up by several glasses, over each loaf; be sure that the cloth does not touch the dough. Let bread rise in a warm spot for 1½ hours.

Bake 20 minutes in 375-degree oven. Remove from oven and again brush the tops with egg white slightly beaten with water. Then bake another 20 minutes.

Cool on wire racks in a drafty spot—important so that bread will not be soggy.

Breads

Bagels

Preheat oven to: 375 degrees
Utensils needed: Electric mixer with dough
  hook; Large bowl, greased; Large cast-iron
  skillet; Cookie sheet, greased
Baking time: Approximately 20 minutes
Quantity: 1 dozen

6 cups lukewarm water	¼ cup sugar
2 tablespoons melted unsalted butter	2 packages yeast
5 cups all-purpose flour	1 large egg white
1 tablespoon salt (optional or to taste)	1 tablespoon cold water
	¼ cup sesame seeds, poppy seeds, or coarse salt (optional)

Mix 1 ¼ cups lukewarm water and melted butter.

Place 3 cups flour, 2 tablespoons sugar, 1 teaspoon salt and yeast in mixing bowl. Add water-butter mixture and beat until well blended. Gradually add remaining flour to make a stiff dough. Beat for 5 minutes.

Remove dough from bowl and place in a large greased bowl. Lightly cover and let rise for 1 hour in a warm, draft-free spot.

Punch dough down. Cover and let set for 20 minutes.

Pour remaining water, sugar and salt into a large cast-iron skillet and bring to a simmer over medium heat.

Divide dough into 12 smooth balls. Use your finger to push a neat 1-inch hole in the center of each ball to make a bagel shape.

Drop 4 bagels at a time into simmering water. Simmer for 3 minutes. Turn over and cook for 3 additional minutes. Turn again and immediately remove from water. Drain on racks covered with a thick layer of paper towel. Repeat process with remaining bagels.

Slightly beat egg white with 1 tablespoon cold water. Set aside.

Place drained bagels on greased cookie sheet. Brush with egg white (and sprinkle with optional seeds or salt, if desired). Bake at 375 degrees for approximately 20 minutes or until lightly browned. Cool on wire racks.

© Steven Mark Needham/Envision

☆ Cuban Bread

Utensils needed: Electric mixer with dough
  hook; 1 baking sheet
Baking time: 40 to 45 minutes
Quantity: 2 loaves

1 package yeast
2 cups lukewarm
  water
1¼ tablespoons salt
  (optional or to
  taste)
1 tablespoon sugar

6 to 7 cups sifted all-
  purpose flour
Approximately ½
  cup cornmeal
¼ cup sesame seeds
boiling water

Dissolve yeast in lukewarm water in large mixing bowl. Add the salt and sugar and stir until dissolved. Add flour one cup at a time, beating well after each addition, until you have added enough to make a smooth dough.

Cover the dough with a towel and set in a warm place to rise until double in size, about 1 ½ hours. Then place on a floured board and shape into 2 loaves, either long or round.

Sprinkle baking sheet heavily with cornmeal. Place loaves on baking sheet and allow to rise for 5 minutes more. Slash the tops, brush with water and sprinkle with sesame seeds.

Place in a *cold* oven, set the oven for 400 degrees and put a pan of boiling water on the bottom shelf. Bake at 400 degrees for 40 to 45 minutes or until tops of loaves are lightly browned. Remove to wire racks to cool.

Tea Breads

Boston Brown Bread

Preheat oven to: 350 degrees
Utensils needed: Electric mixer; 6 gold-lined
  No. 303 tin cans
Baking time: 50 minutes

2 cups boiling water
½ pound raisins
2 teaspoons baking
  soda
2 tablespoons
  unsalted butter

2 cups sugar
2 large eggs
4 cups sifted flour
¼ teaspoon salt
  (optional or to
  taste)

2 teaspoons pure
  vanilla extract

1 cup chopped
  walnuts

In a bowl pour the boiling water over the raisins and baking soda. Mix together and let cool to room temperature.

Cream the butter and sugar together. Add the eggs and mix well. Add the flour, salt, vanilla and chopped nuts. Add the raisin mixture.

Fill the 6 cans about half full. Bake at 350 degrees for 50 minutes, or until breads pull away from sides of cans. When done, let stand in cans for 5 to 10 minutes. Then remove from cans and let cool completely on wire racks.

© Steven Mark Needham/Envision

Whole-Wheat Tea Bread

Preheat oven to: 350 degrees
Utensils needed: Electric mixer; 1 8-inch loaf
pan, greased and floured
Baking time: 55 minutes

1 cup sifted flour
2 teaspoons baking
cinnamon
¼ teaspoon ground
nutmeg
¼ teaspoon ground
allspice
½ cup whole-wheat
flour
¼ cup unsalted
butter

¾ cup sugar
2 eggs
⅔ cup milk
½ teaspoon pure
vanilla extract
½ cup chopped
walnuts

Sift together flour, baking powder, cinnamon, nutmeg and allspice. Stir in whole-wheat flour.

In a separate bowl, cream together the butter and sugar. Add the eggs separately, beating well after each addition.

Add the sifted dry ingredients alternately with the milk and vanilla to the creamed butter mixture. Beat well. Stir in nuts. Pour into prepared pan.

Bake at 350 degrees for 55 minutes or until lightly browned. Cool 10 minutes and remove from pan. Place on wire rack.

Pumpkin Tea Bread

Preheat oven to: 325 degrees
Utensils needed: Electric mixer; 2 9-inch loaf
pans, greased and floured
Baking time: Approximately 1 hour

2 cups sugar
1 cup vegetable oil
3 large eggs, lightly
beaten
2 cups canned
pumpkin
3 cups sifted flour
1 teaspoon baking
soda
¾ teaspoon baking
powder

2 teaspoons ground
cinnamon
1½ teaspoons ground
nutmeg
1 teaspoon ground
cloves
½ teaspoon ground
mace
1 teaspoon ground
ginger

Blend the sugar and oil well with an electric mixer. Then, as you continue beating, add the eggs one at a time, and beat until light. Add the pumpkin. Mix well. Sift the flour, baking soda, baking powder and spices into the creamed mixture. Beat at low speed until blended.

Pour batter into prepared pans and bake at 325 degrees for approximately 1 hour, or until lightly browned. When done, leave in pans for 15 minutes; then remove from pans and cool on wire racks before serving.

Butterscotch Tea Bread

Preheat oven to: 350 degrees
Utensils needed: Electric mixer; 1 9-inch loaf pan, greased and floured
Baking time: Approximately 1 hour

1 large egg, lightly beaten	½ teaspoon baking powder
1 cup firmly packed brown sugar	1 cup buttermilk
1 tablespoon softened unsalted butter	1 cup broken pecan meats
¾ teaspoon baking soda	
2 cups flour	

Beat together thoroughly the egg, brown sugar and butter. Sift together the flour, baking soda and baking powder. Add to egg mixture alternately with the buttermilk. Stir in nuts.

Pour into prepared pan and bake at 350 degrees for about 1 hour or until lightly browned. Remove from pan and cool on wire rack.

© Brian Leatart

Zucchini Tea Bread

Preheat oven to: 350 degrees
Utensils needed: Electric mixer; 2 9-inch loaf pans, greased and floured
Baking time: Approximately 50 minutes

3 large eggs	2 cups flour
1 cup white sugar	½ teaspoon baking powder
½ cup light-brown sugar	2 teaspoons baking soda
¾ cups vegetable oil	2 teaspoons ground cinnamon
2 cups well-drained grated zucchini	
1½ cups chopped pecans	

Beat eggs until light and fluffy. Add sugars and beat until very smooth and thick. Blend in oil. Add zucchini and nuts and stir to mix.

Sift in all dry ingredients and blend well.

Pour into prepared pans and bake at 350 degrees for approximately 50 minutes or until lightly browned. Cool for 10 minutes and remove from pan. Place on wire rack to finish cooling.

Fruit Breads

Apricot Bread

Preheat oven to: 350 degrees
Utensils needed: Electric mixer; 1 9-inch loaf
pan, greased and floured
Baking time: Approximately 50 minutes

½ cup chopped dried
apricots
½ cup seedless raisins
grated rind of 1 large
orange
juice of 1 large
orange
boiling water
1 teaspoon baking
soda
¾ cup sugar

2 tablespoons melted
unsalted butter
1 teaspoon pure
vanilla extract
1 large egg, lightly
beaten
2¼ cups sifted flour
2 teaspoons baking
powder
¾ cup chopped
nutmeats

Place apricots, raisins and grated rind in mixing bowl. Place orange juice in measuring cup and add boiling water to make 1 cup liquid. Add to fruit. Stir in baking soda, sugar, melted butter and vanilla. Stir in beaten egg. Sift in remaining dry ingredients and stir. Blend in nutmeats.

Pour into prepared pan and bake at 350 degrees for about 50 minutes or until lightly browned. Turn upside down on wire rack to cool.

Annie's Orange-Nut Bread

Preheat oven to: 350 degrees
Utensils needed: Electric mixer; 1 9-inch loaf
pan, greased and floured
Baking time: Approximately 55 minutes

1 cup finely chopped
fresh orange peel
2¼ cups sifted
enriched flour
¾ cup sugar
1 tablespoon baking
powder

1 cup chopped
walnuts
2 beaten large eggs
1 cup milk
3 tablespoons
unsalted melted
butter

To prepare orange peel: With a sharp knife, cut peel from 2 very large oranges into thin strips. Lay several strips together on cutting board and chop fine. You may need an extra orange.

Sift together flour, sugar and baking powder. Add orange peel and chopped walnuts.

In a separate bowl, combine eggs, milk and melted butter. Add the egg mixture to the dry ingredients quickly, stirring just until flour is moistened.

Pour into prepared pan and bake at 350 degrees for about 55 minutes or until lightly browned. Remove from pan and cool on wire rack.

Cranberry Bread

Preheat oven to: 350 degrees
Utensils needed: Electric mixer; 1 9-inch loaf
pan, greased and floured
Baking time: 50 minutes

2 cups sifted flour	½ cup chopped
¾ cup sugar	walnuts
1½ teaspoons baking	1 teaspoon grated
powder	fresh orange peel
½ teaspoon baking	1 large egg
soda	¾ cup fresh orange
1 cup coarsely	juice
chopped	2 tablespoons
cranberries	vegetable oil

Sift together the flour, sugar, baking powder and
baking soda. Stir in cranberries, nuts and orange
peel. In another bowl combine the egg, orange
juice and vegetable oil. Add to the flour-fruit mixture. Stir until just moistened.

Pour into prepared pan. Bake at 350 degrees for
50 minutes or until lightly browned. Remove from
pan and cool on wire rack.

Super Date-Nut Bread

Preheat oven to: 325 degrees
Utensils needed: Electric mixer; 3 6-inch loaf
pans, greased and floured

© Bill Margerin/FPG International

Baking time: 10 minutes at 325 degrees;
approximately 30 minutes at 350 degrees

1 pound whole pitted	1 large egg, lightly
dates	beaten
1 teaspoon baking	1 teaspoon pure
soda	vanilla extract
1¼ cups boiling	2 cups sifted flour
water	1½ cups large walnut
1 tablespoon butter	pieces
¾ cup sugar	

Place dates in mixing bowl. Sprinkle with the soda.
Pour the boiling water over the dates. Stir. Add the
butter and mix until it melts. Stir in the sugar. Mix
until it begins to dissolve. Add the lightly beaten
egg and vanilla. Mix well. Sift in the 2 cups sifted
flour and beat well with a wooden spoon. Stir in
the walnut pieces.

Pour batter into prepared pans. Bake at 325
degrees for the first 10 minutes; then raise oven
temperature to 350 degrees and continue baking
for about 30 minutes more.

Remove from pans and cool on wire racks.

Breads

Bettye's Favorite Banana Bread

Preheat oven to: 350 degrees
Utensils needed: Electric mixer; 1 9-inch loaf pan, greased and floured
Baking time: Approximately 1 hour

2 large eggs	3 mashed bananas
⅔ cup sugar	1¾ cups sifted flour
⅓ cup softened unsalted butter	2 teaspoons baking powder

¼ teaspoon baking soda	1 cup large walnut pieces
1 teaspoon pure vanilla extract	

Cream the butter and sugar until light and fluffy. Add eggs and beat well. Add the bananas. Blend well.

Sift together the flour, baking powder and baking soda. Gradually add to the batter. Mix well. Stir in the vanilla and the walnuts.

Pour into prepared pan and bake at 350 degrees for about 1 hour or until lightly browned. Remove from pan and cool on wire rack.

Other Delectables

Sweet Potato Biscuits

Preheat oven to: 400 degrees
Utensils needed: Electric mixer; Rolling pin; Cookie sheet, ungreased
Baking time: Approximately 20 minutes
Quantity: About 2 dozen

1 cup mashed sweet potatoes	½ teaspoon ground cinnamon
2 tablespoons dark brown sugar	dash ground nutmeg
½ cup melted unsalted butter	½ teaspoon baking soda
2 cups flour	¾ cup buttermilk (or sour milk)
2 teaspoons baking powder	

Beat together the sweet potatoes, sugar and butter until well-blended.

Sift together flour, baking powder, cinnamon and nutmeg.

Dissolve baking soda in buttermilk.

Add dry ingredients and buttermilk to potatoes.

Mix until soft dough is formed. DO NOT OVER-BEAT.

Place dough on floured surface and roll out to ½ inch thick. Cut out with a biscuit cutter and place on ungreased cookie sheet. Bake at 400 degrees for approximately 20 minutes or until lightly browned. Cool on wire rack.

Scones

Preheat oven to: 425 degrees
Utensils needed: Food processor; Cookie sheet,
* ungreased*
Baking time: Approximately 12 minutes
Quantity: 1 dozen

2¼ cups flour	*½ cup unsalted*
¼ cup sugar	* butter, chilled*
2 teaspoons baking	*1 large egg*
* powder*	*¾ cup sour cream or*
½ teaspoon baking	* buttermilk*
* soda*	*½ cup currants*

Sift 2 cups flour, 2 tablespoons sugar, baking powder and baking soda into food processor bowl fitted with plastic blade. Add butter cut into small pieces.

Using quick off-and-on turns, cut in butter until mixture resembles fine crumbs.

Lightly beat egg into sour cream (or buttermilk) and quickly blend into crumb mixture. DO NOT OVERBEAT.

Remove from food processor bowl and mix in currants.

Divide dough in half, sprinkle ¼ cup flour on a clean surface and cut each dough piece into a 6- or 7-inch circle about ½ inch thick. Cut each circle into wedges with a well-floured knife.

Place on ungreased cookie sheet about 1 inch apart and sprinkle tops with remaining sugar. Bake at 425 degrees for approximately 12 minutes or until lightly browned.

Breads

© J. Trefethen/FPG International

Mixed-Grain Muffins

Preheat oven to: 400 degrees
Utensils needed: 2 12-cup muffin pans, greased
Baking time: Approximately 20 minutes

1 cup all-purpose flour	2 tablespoons shelled pumpkin seeds
1 cup whole-wheat flour	2 tablespoons ground raw peanuts
1 cup coarsely ground cornmeal	1 tablespoon baking powder
½ cup unsweetened wheat germ	½ teaspoon baking soda
¼ cup oatmeal	2 large eggs
2 tablespoons sesame seeds	1¼ cup plain yogurt
	1½ cup buttermilk

Mix all ingredients together until just moistened. Add additional buttermilk if batter seems dry.

Fill each greased muffin cup ¾ full and bake at 400 degrees for approximately 20 minutes or until golden brown. Cool on wire rack.

☆ Jalapeño Corn Muffins

Preheat oven to: 425 degrees
Utensils needed: 1 12-cup muffin pan, greased
Baking time: Approximately 25 minutes

1 cup yellow cornmeal	1 teaspoon cracked black pepper
1 cup all-purpose flour	¼ teaspoon baking soda
1 teaspoon sugar	1 fresh seeded and minced jalapeño pepper
1 teaspoon baking powder	1 egg
½ teaspoon salt (optional or to taste)	

½ cup plain low-fat yogurt
½ cup half-and-half

½ cup melted bacon fat or vegetable shortening

Mix cornmeal, flour, sugar, baking powder, salt, pepper and baking soda. Stir in jalapeño.

Blend together melted bacon fat (or shortening), egg, yogurt and half-and-half. Stir into dry mixture until just barely combined.

Fill each greased muffin cup ¾ full and bake at 425 degrees for approximately 25 minutes or until golden brown.

Flour Tortillas

Utensils needed: Electric mixer; Cast-iron skillet, lightly greased
Cooking time: Approximately 5 minutes
Quantity: 1½ dozen

4 cups all-purpose flour
1 teaspoon salt
½ teaspoon baking powder

2 tablespoons vegetable shortening
2 cups hot water

Sift together flour, salt and baking powder. Cut in shortening until mixture resembles a coarse meal. Beat in hot water and continue beating for approximately 10 minutes or until dough is very elastic.

Divide dough into approximately 18 equal pieces, each about the size of a golf ball. Roll each out on a lightly floured surface to form a very thin circle 8 inches in diameter. Keep turning the dough to form a perfect circle shape.

Cook, one at a time, in a very hot greased cast-iron skillet over medium heat until light brown on both sides, about 2 minutes per side. Pat down with a spatula to keep bubbles from rising. Cool on wire rack.

Place waxed paper between each tortilla when freezing.

Homemade Butter

Utensils needed: Electric blender or food processor
Quantity: About 1 cup (approximately ½ pound)

1 cup heavy cream
½ cup ice water
2 large ice cubes, chopped

salt to taste (optional)

Place cream in electric blender or food processor fitted with the plastic blade. Cover and whip at highest speed. When cream is whipped, add water and chopped ice cubes. Cover and blend at highest speed at least 2 minutes or until all cream has turned to butter particles.

Pour contents of blender into a sieve to drain. When all water has drained through, place butter in a small bowl. Add salt, if desired, and knead with a wooden spoon until butter is smooth. Place in covered butter crock or plastic container in the refrigerator.

NOTE: For variety, you may add to the butter a clove of garlic, a tablespoon of grated orange or lemon peel or 1 tablespoon of any chopped fresh herb you wish. Add the flavoring when you add the water and ice.

Cookies

© Amy Reichman,/Envision

There is nothing friendlier than a filled cookie jar given as a gift. Almost everyone has a favorite cookie, but we hope that you will find new favorites among the recipes we have included here.

Cookies are usually the easiest of homemade goodies. Nonstick cookie sheets make baking quicker and cleaner than ever. If you don't use these, you can line other types with greased aluminum foil, which can be prepared in advance. If you follow the directions closely and use prepared baking sheets, you will find cookie baking a breeze.

An assortment of cookie cutters and a cookie press will greatly enhance your repertoire. You can order any one of a large variety of cookie cutters from gour-met stores or mail-order kitchenware catalogues, or you can make your own patterns using heavy cardboard. Illustrations in children's coloring books offer a variety of ideas for cookie shapes. Different-sized jars, glasses or lids can be used. You can even cut out the shape of your hand.

Most of our cookie recipes call for unsalted butter. You can, of course, substitute salted butter or margarine, but this will change the taste, and occasionally the texture, of your cookie. For some cookies this will not matter, but rich cookies (those with few ingredients beyond butter, sugar and flour) demand the strong butter flavor. If you wish to see which you prefer, Shortbread is the best cookie to experiment with; margarine, unsalted butter and salted butter will give you three entirely different results. Cookies made with margarine will keep longer than those made with butter.

Most cookies are lifted from the baking sheet immediately upon removal from the oven. They are best cooled on wire cake racks. The exception is bar cookies, which are cut and cooled directly in their baking pan. If you use a disposable foil baking pan, bar cookies may also be given as a gift while still in the pan.

Unless otherwise specified, cookies may be frozen either unbaked or baked. (Exception: It is best not to freeze dough made with vegetable oil, as freezing will make the dough crumbly.) Pressed or cut-out cookies may be formed into the desired shapes, frozen on a cookie sheet, then removed and placed in layers in freezer wrap or a plastic bag for further freezer storage. Thaw unbaked dough thoroughly before using. Frozen baked cookies should be placed to thaw on paper toweling so that the moisture will be absorbed and the cookies will remain crisp.

A batch of homemade cookies to be given as a gift can be placed in almost any covered container. If they are packed in a box, it is best to place them in layers separated by tissue, foil, waxed paper or cellophane. Brightly colored tissue paper is a festive addition. A fruitcake tin or any reusable plastic container can be made into an attractive package. A large coffee can (or any large can with a plastic lid) can be painted and decorated with stick-on decals or covered with adhesive-backed decorating paper and used as a cookie container. Restaurant-sized mayonnaise or pickle jars make superb cookie jars when decorated.

Innumerable kitchen utensils can be purchased to serve as containers for cookie gifts: a large colander, a flour sifter, cookie sheets, mixing bowls—anything large enough to hold at least 1 pound of cookies. These are wonderful items for a new household or a bachelor or for shower gifts. A set of mixing bowls filled with cookies and wrapped in colored cellophane with a wooden spoon, a pastry brush or a spatula tied in the ribbon makes a charming gift package. If you are an antique- or junk-shop browser, you can always find old crocks or jars that are great for cookies.

For most children, homemade cookies are a special treat. A sandpail, a lunch box or a plastic dump truck is an inexpensive and appropriate container for a cookie gift to a child. This kind of gift is particularly appealing to a child recuperating from an illness.

All the cookie recipes given are good keepers. If you plan to send a batch of cookies through the mail, do not select

those that are marked fragile. Check page 142 for additional hints on mailing packaging cookies.

We have divided the cookies into six categories: Bar, Drop, Molded, Refrigerator, Cookie-Press and Cutout. At the end of this section we have included a recipe for Icing which may be used on any homemade cookie that calls for decoration (see page 53).

Bar Cookies

Easy Lebkuchen

Preheat oven to: 375 degrees
Utensils needed: Electric mixer; 2 cookie
 sheets, greased
Baking time: 25 minutes
Quantity: 6 dozen
Storing: Airtight container for 4 weeks

4 large eggs
2 cups tightly packed
 light-brown sugar
2 cups sifted all-
 purpose flour
1 teaspoon cinnamon
¾ cup finely chopped
 pecans
¼ cup finely chopped
 citron
2 tablespoons finely
 chopped candied
 orange peel

Beat the eggs with the sugar until light.

Mix flour and cinnamon with nuts, citron and orange peel. Combine flour mixture with egg mixture, blending well.

Spread dough onto prepared cookie sheets. Bake at 375 degrees for 25 minutes or until lightly browned. When cooled, cut into strips approximately 5 inches x 1 inch.

Date Logs

Preheat oven to: 350 degrees
Utensils needed: Electric mixer; 1 13 x 9 x 2-
 inch pan, greased and floured
Baking time: About 25 minutes
Quantity: 6 dozen
Storing: Individually plastic-wrapped in
 airtight container for 2 weeks.

3 large eggs
1 cup sugar
1½ tablespoons fresh
 orange juice
1 teaspoon fresh
 lemon juice
¾ cup sifted all-
 purpose flour
½ teaspoon baking
 powder
1 cup chopped pitted
 dates
¼ cup chopped
 candied orange
 peel
1 cup chopped
 macadamia nuts
granulated sugar

Beat eggs until foamy and light. Gradually add the sugar and continue beating until fluffy and thick. Stir in the fruit juices.

Sift together the flour and baking powder and fold into the egg mixture. Gently fold in the dates, peel and nuts, making sure all ingredients are blended. Pour into prepared pan and spread the mixture evenly.

Bake at 350 degrees for about 25 minutes or until toothpick inserted comes out clean. Cool in pan on wire rack at least 15 minutes. While still warm, cut lengthwise into 9 strips and crosswise into 8 strips, making 72 pieces. Remove from pan one at a time, and roll logs in granulated sugar. Finish cooling on wire rack.

© Steven Mark Needham/Envision

Edna's Brownies

Preheat oven to: 350 degrees
Utensils needed: Electric mixer; 1 8-inch-square pan, greased and floured
Baking time: About 25 minutes
Quantity: About 3 dozen
Storing: Individually plastic-wrapped in airtight container for 10 days

½ cup unsalted butter	½ cup sifted all-purpose flour
1 cup sugar	5 tablespoons cocoa
2 large eggs	½ cup chopped walnuts
1 teaspoon pure vanilla extract	

Cream the butter and sugar until light and fluffy. Beat in the eggs and vanilla.

Sift the flour and cocoa into the creamed mixture. Mix well. Stir in the chopped nuts and pour into prepared pan.

Bake at 350 degrees for about 25 minutes or until toothpick inserted comes out clean. Cut into squares while still warm, but leave in pan until brownies are cold.

Praline Cookies

Preheat oven to: 325 degrees
Utensils needed: Electric mixer; 1 cookie sheet, greased
Baking time: 25 minutes
Quantity: Approximately 3 dozen
Storing: Individually plastic-wrapped in loosely covered container for 10 days

½ cup unsalted butter	1 teaspoon pure vanilla extract
1½ cups light-brown sugar	1½ cups sifted all-purpose flour
1 large egg	1 cup coarsely chopped pecans

Cream together butter and sugar until light and fluffy. Add the egg and mix thoroughly. Add the vanilla, flour and nuts. Mix well.

Spread the mixture over the prepared pan with a spatula, extending the dough as closely to the edges of the pan as possible. Bake at 325 degrees for 25 minutes or until lightly browned. When cool, cut into squares.

 Drop Cookies

Anise Caps

Preheat oven to: 350 degrees
Utensils needed: Electric mixer; At least 2
  cookie sheets, generously greased
Setting time: At least 12 hours
Baking time: 5 to 6 minutes
Quantity: About 4 dozen
Storing: Uncovered container for 2 weeks. Do
  not freeze or refrigerate.

2 large eggs	¼ teaspoon baking
1 cup superfine sugar	powder
¼ teaspoon anise	anise seed for cookie
extract	tops
1½ cups sifted all-	
purpose flour	

Beat eggs until foamy. Gradually add the sugar and beat until very thick. When the mixture piles softly, add the anise extract. Sift the dry ingredients into the egg mixture and blend lightly.

Drop by the teaspoon 1–1½ inches apart onto the prepared pans. Sprinkle the top of each cookie with a small amount of anise seed.

Important: Before baking, these cookies must set at least 12 hours in a cool place. Do not cover them, and do not place them in the refrigerator.

When cookies have set, bake at 350 degrees for about 5 or 6 minutes or until faintly brown. Remove from pan and cool on wire racks.

Lizzies

Preheat oven to: 325 degrees
Utensils needed: Electric mixer; At least 2
  cookie sheets, greased
Baking time: About 15 minutes
Quantity: 8 dozen
Storing: Airtight container for 3 weeks

3 cups seedless dark raisins	2 large eggs
½ cups bourbon (or fresh orange juice)	1½ teaspoons ground cinnamon
¼ cup softened unsalted butter	½ teaspoon ground nutmeg
½ cup light-brown sugar	½ teaspoons ground cloves
1½ cups sifted all-purpose flour	2 cups whole pecan halves
1 teaspoon baking soda	1 cup diced citron
	2 cups whole candied red cherries

Place the raisins and bourbon (or fresh orange juice) in a bowl. Stir and set aside for 1 hour.

Cream the butter and sugar until light and fluffy. Add the eggs; beat until well-blended and fluffy. Sift together the flour, baking soda and spices. Add gradually to the creamed mixture alternately with the raisin mixture. Stir in the pecans, citron and cherries. Blend well.

Drop by the teaspoonful onto prepared cookie

sheets. Bake at 325 degrees for 15 minutes or until lightly browned. Remove from pan and cool on wire racks.

Crybabies

Preheat oven to: 350 degrees
Utensils needed: Electric mixer; At least 2
  cookie sheets, greased
Baking time: 12 to 15 minutes
Quantity: About 6 dozen
Storing: Loosely covered container for 10 days

1 cup softened unsalted butter	ginger
1 cup sugar	1 cup strong hot coffee
1 cup molasses	2 teaspoons baking soda
2½ cups sifted all-purpose flour (more if needed)	1 cup seedless dark raisins
2 teaspoons ground cinnamon	1 cup chopped walnuts
½ teaspoon ground	

Cream butter and sugar until light and fluffy. Beat in the molasses.

Sift together the flour, cinnamon and ginger. Add to creamed mixture alternately with the hot coffee, in which you have dissolved 2 teaspoons baking soda. Stir in the raisins and nuts. Drop by the teaspoonful 1–1½ inches apart onto prepared cookie sheets. Bake at 350 degrees for 12 to 15 minutes or until lightly browned. Remove from pan and cool on wire racks.

Christmas Hermits

Preheat oven to: 375 degrees
Utensils needed: Electric mixer; At least 2
  cookie sheets, greased
Baking time: About 20 minutes
Quantity: About 10 dozen
Storing: Airtight container for 3 weeks

1 cup softened unsalted butter	grated rind of 1 medium orange
3 cups light-brown sugar	1 teaspoon ground nutmeg
4 tablespoons milk	1 teaspoon ground cinnamon
4 large eggs	
3 teaspoons baking powder	
6 cups sifted all-purpose flour	
2 cups seedless raisins	
2 cups currants	
1 cup chopped nutmeats	

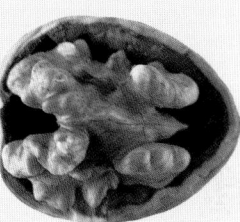

Cream butter and sugar until light and fluffy. Beat in milk and eggs.

Sift the baking powder with 3 cups of the flour. Add to the creamed mixture. Blend well. Add the raisins, currants, nutmeats and orange rind and mix well.

Sift spices with the balance of the flour and add to the mixture. Blend together.

Drop by the teaspoonful 1–1½ inches apart onto prepared cookie sheets. Bake at 375 degrees for about 20 minutes or until light brown. Remove from pan and cool on wire racks.

Molded Cookies

Greek Kourabiedes

Preheat oven to: 350 degrees
Utensils needed: Electric mixer; At least 2
   cookie sheets, greased
Baking time: Approximately 18 minutes
Quantity: About 4 dozen
Storing: Airtight container for 1 week or
   refrigerated for longer storage

1 pound unsalted butter, at room temperature	1 large egg yolk
¾ cup unsifted confectioner's sugar	1½ tablespoons brandy
	4 cups sifted all-purpose flour
	confectioner's sugar

Cream butter until it is extremely light. Add ¾ cup confectioner's sugar and beat until mixture is very fluffy and pale in color. Beat in egg yolk and brandy.

Gradually add flour. Blend to make a soft dough that will shape into balls without sticking to your hands. Make the balls about 1 inch in diameter and place on prepared cookie sheets about 2 inches apart.

Bake at 350 degrees for about 18 minutes or until lightly browned. Cool slightly on cookie sheet; then transfer to waxed paper and dust with confectioner's sugar. Finish cooling on wire racks.

Chocolate Pixies

Chilling time: ½ hour
Preheat oven to: 375 degrees
Utensils needed: Electric mixer; At least 2
   cookie sheets, greased
Baking time: About 12 minutes
Quantity: About 4 dozen
Storing: Airtight container for 2 weeks

4 squares unsweetened chocolate, melted	4 large eggs
½ cup unsalted butter	2 cups sifted all-purpose flour
1½ cups sugar	2 teaspoons baking powder
2 teaspoons pure vanilla extract	½ cup chopped pecans
	confectioner's sugar

Melt the chocolate in top of double boiler and let cool.

Cream the butter, sugar and vanilla until light and fluffy. Beat in the eggs. Continue beating and add the cool, melted chocolate.

Sift together the flour and baking powder. Add to the creamed mixture and blend thoroughly. Stir in the chopped pecans. Chill about ½ hour.

When chilled, roll dough into 1-inch balls. Roll each ball in confectioner's sugar.

Place on prepared cookie sheets at least 2 inches

apart. Bake at 375 degrees for about 12 minutes or until lightly browned. Cool slightly on cookie sheets. Remove and finish cooling on wire racks.

© Steven Mark Needham/Envision

Fingers

Preheat oven to: 300 degrees
Utensils needed: Electric mixer; At least 2 cookie sheets, greased
Baking time: 20 to 25 minutes
Quantity: About 7 dozen
Storing: Airtight container for 2 weeks

1 cup softened unsalted butter	2 cups sifted all-purpose flour
1 cup sugar	1½ teaspoons pure vanilla extract
1 cup finely ground macadamia nuts (or hazelnuts)	confectioner's sugar

Cream butter and sugar until light and fluffy. Work in the nuts, flour and vanilla with a pastry blender or your fingers. Work with hands until dough holds together. If mixture is not holding, add about 1

tablespoon of ice water.

Shape each heaping teaspoon of dough into a "finger" by rolling on a board or between your palms. Place fingers on prepared cookie sheets at least 2 inches apart.

Bake at 300 degrees for 20 to 25 minutes or until lightly browned. Place baked cookies on sheet of waxed paper or foil, dust with confectioner's sugar and cool on wire racks.

Wedding Cakes

Preheat oven to: 350 degrees
Utensils needed: Electric mixer; 1 cookie sheet, greased
Baking time: 15 to 20 minutes
Quantity: 3 dozen
Storing: Individually plastic-wrapped in airtight container for 5 days

½ pound melted unsalted butter	2 cups finely chopped pecans or walnuts
8 tablespoons confectioner's sugar	1 teaspoon pure vanilla extract
2 cups sifted all-purpose flour	confectioner's sugar

Mix together melted butter and 8 tablespoons sugar. Add flour, nuts and vanilla. Roll into teaspoon-sized balls. Place on cookie sheet and bake at 350 degrees for 15 to 20 minutes or until lightly browned. While still warm, roll each ball in confectioner's sugar. Cool on wire racks.

Refrigerator Cookies

Italian Anise Cookies

Chilling time: 1 hour
Preheat oven to: 350 degrees
Utensils needed: Electric mixer; At least 2
  cookie sheets, greased
Baking time: 30 minutes—first time. About 5
  minutes—second time
Quantity: About 6 dozen
Storing: Airtight container for 4 weeks. Do
  not freeze

3 large eggs
1 cup sugar
¼ cup melted
  unsalted butter
2 cups sifted all-
  purpose flour
2 teaspoons baking
  powder
1 teaspoon anise
  extract
1 teaspoon anise seed
½ cup chopped
  almonds

Beat the eggs and sugar until creamy. Add the melted butter and mix well. Sift the flour and baking powder together into the egg mixture. Beat until well-blended and thick. Add the anise extract and seed and the chopped nuts. If the dough seems too soft to roll, add a bit more flour.

Form the dough into rolls about 2 inches thick. Chill in refrigerator about 1 hour. When chilled, bake the whole rolls at 350 degrees for 30 minutes or until quite firm and lightly browned. Remove from oven and slice diagonally on the cookie sheets. Put back in the oven for about 5 minutes. Remove from pans and cool on wire racks.

Spice Cookies

Chilling Time: 12 or more hours
Preheat oven to: 325 degrees
Utensils needed: Electric mixer; 2 cookie
  sheets, greased
Baking time: 10 to15 minutes
Quantity: 10 dozen
Storing: Plastic bags tied, for 2 weeks.

1 cup light brown
  sugar
1 cup white sugar
1½ cups melted
  unsalted butter
3 large eggs

2 teaspoons baking
  soda
1 teaspoon ground
  cinnamon
½ teaspoon ground
  cloves

1 cup chopped nuts
4⅓ cups sifted all-
  purpose flour

½ teaspoon ground
  nutmeg

Mix together the brown and white sugars and melted butter. Add eggs one at a time, mixing thoroughly after each addition. Add chopped nuts.

Sift together flour, baking soda and spices. Add sifted dry ingredients to sugar-shortening mixture and blend well.

Form dough into long rolls and wrap in waxed paper. Chill in refrigerator at least 12 hours.

Slice about ¼ inch thick. Place on cookie sheets and bake at 325 degrees for 10 to 15 minutes or until light brown. Remove from pans and cool on wire racks.

© McFarland/FPG International

Coconut Cookies

Chilling time: 12 hours or more
Preheat oven to: 325 degrees
Utensils needed: Electric mixer; 2 cookie
  sheets, greased
Baking time: 10 to 15 minutes
Quantity: 6 dozen
Storing: Plastic bags tied, for 2 weeks

2 cups light brown
  sugar
⅔ cup unsalted
  butter
2 large eggs, beaten
1 teaspoon pure
  vanilla extract
1 teaspoon baking
  soda
1 tablespoon hot
  water

3 cups sifted all-
  purpose flour
1 teaspoon cream of
  tartar
2 cups coconut,
  flaked

Cream together butter and sugar until light and fluffy. Add eggs and vanilla. Dissolve baking soda in hot water and add to mixture.

Sift together flour and cream of tartar. Add sifted dry ingredients to creamed mixture. Blend well. Add coconut and mix until just blended.

Form dough into long rolls and wrap in waxed paper. Chill in refrigerator at least 12 hours.

Slice about ¼ inch thick. Place on cookie sheets and bake at 325 degrees for 10 to 15 minutes or until lightly browned. Remove from pans and cool on wire racks.

Cookies

Jam Pastries

Chilling time: 6 hours or overnight
Preheat oven to: 400 degrees
Utensils needed: Food processor; At least 2 ungreased cookie sheets
Baking time: 10 to 15 minutes. Watch closely
Quantity: About 5 dozen
Storing: Loosely covered container in refrigerator for 1 week

¼ pound chilled unsalted margarine

¼ pound chilled unsalted butter

½ pound chilled cream cheese
2 cups sifted flour

jam, jelly, preserves for filling

Cut the margarine, butter and cream cheese into the sifted flour, using the plastic blade in the food processor. Work into a smooth dough. Form into 1-inch balls. Chill at least 6 hours or overnight. (These may also be frozen before baking.)

When chilled, roll out each ball with the cushion of your hand. Fill center of each with desired filling. Fold sides together and press tight. Bake at 400 degrees for 10 to 15 minutes or until a pale golden color. Remove from pans and cool on wire racks before storing.

 Cookie-Press Cookies

Lemon Strips

Preheat oven to: 400 degrees
Utensils needed: Electric mixer; At least 2 cookie sheets, greased; Cookie press with pencil-like tip
Baking time: 6 to 10 minutes
Quantity: About 4 dozen
Storing: In layers in tightly covered container for 2 weeks

½ cup unsalted butter
½ cup sugar
4 large egg whites

1 cup sifted all-purpose flour
1 teaspoon lemon extract
1 teaspoon finely grated lemon rind

Cream butter until light. Add sugar and continue creaming until fluffy. Add egg whites one at a time and mix well. Stir in the sifted flour, blending all together. Add the lemon extract and rind. Mix into dough.

Place dough in cookie press fitted with pencil-like tip. Press onto prepared baking sheets in 3-to-4-inch strips, at least 1 ½ inches apart.

Bake at 400 degrees for 6 to 10 minutes or until lightly browned.

Remove from pans and cool on wire racks.

Chocolate Cheese Cookies

Chilling time: 30 minutes
Preheat oven to: 375 degrees
Utensils needed: Electric mixer; At least 2 ungreased cookie sheets; Cookie press
Baking time: 8 to 10 minutes
Quantity: About 5 dozen
Storing: Loosely covered container for 1 week

1 cup softened unsalted butter	2 squares unsweetened chocolate, melted
1 3-ounce package cream cheese, softened	2½ cups sifted all-purpose flour
1 cup sugar	1 teaspoon baking powder
1 large egg	

Cream together the butter and cream cheese. Add the sugar and beat until light and fluffy. Beat in the egg and melted chocolate. Sift together the flour and baking powder and mix into the creamed mixture. Chill dough for 30 minutes. Pack dough into cookie press and force onto ungreased cookie sheets in desired shapes, 1-1 ½ inches apart. Bake at 375 degrees for 8 to 10 minutes or until lightly browned. Remove from pans and cool on wire racks before storing.

Scotch Shortbread

Preheat oven to: 300 degrees
Utensils needed: Electric mixer; Cookie press and at least 2 ungreased cookie sheets or 2 9-inch cake pans
Baking time: Check after 10 minutes, full time approximately 20 minutes
Quantity: 6 to 8 dozen if made in a cookie press: 18 1-inch wedges if made in cake tins
Storing: Individually plastic-wrapped in loosely covered container for 1 week; covered and refrigerated for 2 weeks

2 cups softened unsalted butter	1 teaspoon pure vanilla extract (optional)
1 cup superfine sugar	
4⅓ cups sifted all-purpose flour	

Cream the butter and sugar together until light and fluffy. Add the flour (and vanilla, if desired) and mix well.

We prefer to make these cookies in a cookie press. An alternative method, however, is to fit the dough into 2 9-inch cake tins with the edges pressed as for a piecrust. Prick with a fork. Bake at 300 degrees for 10 to 20 minutes or until lightly browned. When baked, cut the shortbread into pie-shaped slices as soon as it is removed from the oven. Let cool in pans.

If cookies are made in a press, use shapes desired and place on ungreased cookie sheets. Bake at 300 degrees for 10 to 20 minutes or until edges are lightly browned. Remove from pans and cool on wire racks.

Cookies

Orange Cheese Cookies

Chilling time: At least 15 minutes
Preheat oven to: 400 degrees
Utensils needed: Electric mixer; At least 2
  ungreased cookie sheets; Cookie press
Baking time: 10 to 12 minutes
Quantity: About 5 dozen
Storing: Airtight in refrigerator for 1 week

½ cup softened
  unsalted butter
1 3-ounce package
  cream cheese
⅓ cup sugar
1 large egg yolk

1½ teaspoons orange
  extract
1½ cups sifted all-
  purpose flour
1 teaspoon finely
  grated orange rind

Cream the butter and cream cheese together until well blended. Gradually add sugar until mixture is light and fluffy. Add the egg yolk and flavoring; beat well.

Add flour to creamed mixture by the half cup, beating well after each addition. Stir in grated orange rind.

Chill at least 15 minutes before using.

Force dough through cookie press directly onto the ungreased cookie sheets, 1-1½ inches apart. Keep unused dough in the refrigerator until you are ready for it.

Bake at 400 degrees for 10 to 12 minutes or until lightly browned.

Remove from pans and cool on wire racks.

Cutout Cookies

Black-Walnut Cookies

Preheat oven to: 350 degrees
Utensils needed: Electric mixer; Rolling pin;
  At least 2 cookie sheets, greased; Small
  round cookie cutter dusted with confec-
  tioner's sugar
Baking time: 15 to 18 minutes

Quantity: About 5 dozen
Storing: Airtight container for 10 days

1 cup softened
  unsalted butter
¾ cup superfine
  sugar
1 cup finely ground
  black walnuts

(English walnuts
  may be substituted)
2 cups sifted all-
  purpose flour
confectioner's sugar

Cream the butter until extremely light. Gradually beat in sugar, and mix until fluffy and very pale in color. Stir in the finely ground walnuts, blending well. Gradually sift in flour to make a soft dough.

Place dough on a board dusted with either flour or confectioner's sugar. Roll out about ¼ inch thick. Cut into small rounds with prepared cookie cutter. Place on prepared baking sheets at least ½ inch apart.

Bake at 350 degrees for 15 to 18 minutes or until lightly browned. Cool slightly in pans. Transfer to waxed paper and dust with confectioner's sugar. Finish cooling on wire racks.

Wine Stars

Chilling time: 3 hours
Preheat oven to: 400 degrees
Utensils needed: Electric mixer; Rolling pin; 2 cookie sheets, lightly greased; 2-inch star-shaped cookie cutter

Baking time: 12 minutes
Quantity: 6 dozen
Storing: Individually plastic-wrapped in loosely covered container for 1 week

½ cup soft unsalted butter
1⅓ cups light-brown sugar
1 large egg
½ cup finely chopped blanched almonds
3 cups sifted all-purpose flour
½ teaspoon baking soda
¾ teaspoon ground cinnamon
2 tablespoons red wine or sherry
⅛ teaspoon almond extract

Cream butter and sugar together until light and fluffy. Beat in egg. Stir in almonds.

Sift together flour, baking soda and cinnamon. Add to butter-sugar mixture along with wine or sherry and flavoring.

Chill 3 hours.

On floured board, roll out ¼ inch thick. Cut into stars with cookie cutter.

Place on prepared cookie sheets and bake at 400 degrees for 12 minutes or until lightly browned. Remove from pans and cool on wire racks.

© Floyd Jillson/FPG International

Old-Time Christmas Cutouts

Standing time: Overnight
Preheat oven to: 350 degrees
Utensils needed: Electric mixer; Rolling pin;
*   At least 2 cookie sheets, greased; Cookie*
*   cutters or cardboard patterns*
Baking time: About 8 minutes
Quantity: Hundreds
Storing: Airtight container for 3 weeks

3 cups dark corn syrup	2 tablespoons ground allspice
1 cup plus 4 tablespoons unsalted butter	½ teaspoon ground ginger
1½ cups vegetable shortening or butter	1 pound light-brown sugar
4 pounds sifted all-purpose flour	¼ cup fresh lemon juice
	grated rind of 1 lemon

3 tablespoons ground cinnamon	3½ teaspoons baking soda
3 tablespoons ground cloves	2 tablespoons warm water
1 rounded teaspoon ground cardamom	

Place corn syrup, butter and shortening in heavy saucepan over medium heat. Stir until melted. Set aside, but keep warm.

In a very large mixing bowl, mix the flour, spices and sugar. Blend together.

Gradually pour the warm mixture over the flour mixture. Stir by hand. Mix in the lemon juice and rind. Continue mixing and add the soda dissolved in the warm water. Knead dough well.

Let stand at room temperature overnight.

Roll dough paper-thin and cut into shapes. Place on prepared pans and bake at 350 degrees for about 8 minutes or until lightly browned. Remove from baking pan and cool on wire racks. You may decorate with icing when cooled.

NOTE: These cookies make wonderful Christmas-tree decorations. With a small skewer, pierce a hole about ¼ inch from the top of each cookie before baking.

Sand Tarts

Chilling time: 3 hours
Preheat oven to: 350 degrees
Utensils needed: Electric mixer; Rolling pin;
*   At least 2 lightly greased cookie sheets;*
*   Circle cookie cutter*

Baking time: 6 to 8 minutes
Quantity: About 12 dozen
Storing: Loosely covered container for 1 week

2 cups unsalted
butter
2 cups sugar
2 large eggs
¼ pound finely
ground macadamia
nuts
2 pounds sifted all-
purpose flour

© R. Chandler/FPG International

Cream the butter and sugar until light and fluffy. Beat in the eggs and finely ground macadamia nuts, mixing well. Gradually sift in the flour, stirring by hand until well-blended.

Chill dough at least 3 hours.

Roll out about ⅛ inch thick on lightly floured board. Cut into circles and place on prepared cookie sheets. Keep unused dough chilled.

Bake at 350 degrees for 6 to 8 minutes or until lightly browned. Remove from pans and cool on wire racks.

VARIATION:

Brush the tops of unbaked cookies with lightly beaten egg white and sprinkle with cinnamon sugar before baking.

Icing

Utensils needed: Electric mixer and small mixing bowl. Small bowl for each color
Quantity: About 1½ cups
Do not store.

1½ cups sifted
confectioner's
sugar
1 large egg white

pinch salt
1 teaspoon fresh
lemon juice
food coloring

Place all ingredients except food coloring in small mixing bowl. Beat until well blended on medium speed of electric mixer.

If you wish only one icing color, add food coloring drop by drop until you reach shade desired. For a variety of colors, divide the icing as you wish into small bowls. Mix each color individually.

Use as quickly as possible. If icing sets or gets too thick before you are finished decorating, add water a drop at a time.

NOTE: This icing is good for any cookie that calls for trim or decoration.

Cookies

Chocolate Nut Caramels, Sesame Butter Crunch and Raisin-Peanut Drops

Candy and Nuts

© D. Degroat/FPG International

Except for an occasional batch of fudge, most cooks seem to avoid candy making. As delicious as homemade fudge is, there are many superb varieties of candy to explore. For gift giving, there is nothing more unexpected than homemade candy.

There are two basic methods of preparing candy, thermometer and nonthermometer. Those recipes that do not require a thermometer are usually the easiest and quickest. If you have never tried your hand at candy making, start with an easy recipe (such as Never-Fail Chocolate Fudge). Whichever method you choose, you will find candy making much easier than anticipated, if you follow some basic rules: Always follow the recipe exactly. Do not substitute ingredients until you are a really experienced candy cook. Cook all candy in a heavy saucepan (cast iron is excellent), and use a wooden spoon for stirring.

If you do not own a candy thermometer and are going to make a candy that requires one, we strongly suggest that you purchase one. The cost is not great, and we feel that the investment is well worth it. If this is not possible, keep within reach a small bowl or glass of ice water in which you can test the consistency of the candy.

For the ice-water method of testing, use the following descriptions as your guide:

235–240 degrees—Soft ball	Soft ball is formed when syrup is dropped into water. Ball can be flattened when removed.
245–248 degrees—Firm ball	As above, except that ball cannot be flattened when removed.
250–265 degrees—Hard ball	Hard ball, one that holds its shape but can be molded, is formed when syrup is dropped into water.
270–290 degrees—Soft crack	Hard threads are formed when syrup is dropped into water.
300–310 degrees—Hard crack	Brittle threads are formed when syrup is dropped into water.

Gift containers for homemade candy can be of almost any size or shape. One of the easiest is a 1- or 2-pound can with a snap-on plastic lid (coffee, shortening or nut can). Spray-painted and decorated with stick-on decals, the can may be used over and over. Children's shoe boxes; disposable foil pans; boxes for foil, waxed paper or plastic wrap; frozen-food pans and oatmeal containers are a few other ideas for candy holders. They can be decorated with adhesive-backed decorating paper or gift wrap and ribbons. Candy cups can be ordered through a store in our Shopping Guide, or you can make them yourself with small pieces of aluminum foil. They are very helpful packing aids.

Individually wrapped candy pieces can be packed inside a paper tube (such as those on which paper towels are rolled). With a bit of decoration you can make it look like a firecracker or a candle: Seal the bottom with a small piece of cardboard. Make another circular cover to fit the top, and attach to it either a small piece of white string or a piece of yellow ribbon cut into a flame shape. Cover the roll with red paper, glue tightly, and you will have a charming package.

As with other homemade gifts, the dime store and junk shops provide many unusual containers. Apothecary jars, old soda glasses, and antique bowls, boxes or vases make marvelous containers. Fill them with candy, seal with plastic wrap and tie with a bright ribbon bow. Your candy will look almost too good to eat.

We do not suggest shipping candy long distances, unless by airmail. The temperature changes in shipment are sometimes so drastic that the candy either melts or crumbles, however securely wrapped.

Each candy recipe has storing in-

structions. All candies should be stored in a cool place for a maximum life.

Most of our nut recipes are quick and easy. They make particularly good hostess gifts. Nuts are best packed in a can with a snap-on plastic lid. You can purchase these lids (fitting a No. 303-sized can) in most large dime stores or in the house-wares departments of department stores. We spray-paint several cans at a time and keep stick-on decals handy so that we are always prepared for gift giving.

Nonthermometer Candy

© Jeanetta Ho

Cream ½ cup of butter. Add sugar and liquor alternately, beating until thick and smooth.

Shape mixture into half-teaspoonful-size balls. Press a pecan half on each side of the ball and chill about 20 minutes.

Melt chocolate with 1½ teaspoons of butter. Dip one end of each candy in the chocolate and put on prepared cookie sheet. Chill until firm.

Pecan Bourbon Candy

No cooking
Chilling time: 20 minutes
Utensils needed: Electric mixer or food processor; Cookie sheet covered with waxed paper
Quantity: 2½ pounds
Storing: Individually plastic-wrapped in loosely covered container in refrigerator for 1 week

½ cup unsalted butter	3 cups pecan halves
2 cups confectioner's sugar	8 ounces semisweet chocolate
⅓ cup bourbon (or rum or brandy)	

Butterscotch Nut Drops

Utensils needed: Saucepan
Boiling time: 3 minutes
Quantity: 1¾ pounds
Storing: Individually plastic-wrapped in airtight container for 2 weeks

2 cups sugar	1 teaspoon white vinegar
1 cup light-brown sugar	1 6-ounce package butterscotch pieces
¾ cup water	
¼ cup light corn syrup	1 cup coarsely chopped macadamia nuts

Place both sugars, water, corn syrup and vinegar in saucepan. Bring to full boil, stirring constantly. Boil 3 minutes over high heat without stirring. Remove from heat and add butterscotch pieces, stirring until melted. Add nuts and drop by spoonfuls on ungreased foil (If mixture becomes too thick to drop, add a little hot water, a teaspoon at a time.) Let stand until set.

Raisin-Peanut Drops

Utensils needed: Double boiler
Quantity: About 4 dozen pieces
Storing: Layers in tightly covered container
    for 10 days

12 ounces semisweet chocolate	2 cups seedless raisins
2 14-ounce cans sweetened condensed milk	2 cups chopped unsalted roasted peanuts
1 teaspoon unsalted butter	1 cup miniature marshmallows

Melt the chocolate in top part of double boiler over very hot water. When melted, add the milk and butter. Cook for about 12 minutes or until mixture is quite thick, stirring constantly. Add the raisins, marshmallows and chopped nuts. Stir until well-blended.

Drop by the tablespoonful onto waxed paper or foil. Refrigerate until well set, about 3 hours.

Peppermint Wafers

No cooking
Utensils needed: Electric mixer or food
    processor
Setting time: 12 hours
Quantity: About 1 pound
Storing: Loosely covered container for 10
    days. Do not store different flavors
    together.

1 large egg white	few drops red food coloring
2¾ cups sifted confectioner's sugar	
2 teaspoons softened unsalted butter	
2 teaspoons peppermint extract	

Beat the egg white until foamy. Gradually sift in the confectioner's sugar. Mix well. Add the softened butter, extract and food coloring. Blend.

Roll dough into approximately ¾-inch balls. Place on waxed paper or foil about 1½ inches apart. Flatten with fork tines, making lines go in one direction.

VARIATIONS:

1. For Wintergreen Wafers: Use 2 teaspoons wintergreen extract and green food coloring.

2. For Spearmint Wafers: Use 2 teaspoons spearmint extract and yellow food coloring.

3. For Fruit-flavored Wafers: Use 2 teaspoons fruit extract (orange, lemon, cherry, etc.) and coloring appropriate to fruit.

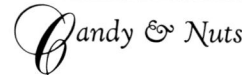

© Bruce K. Nesset

Doris' Applets

Utensils needed: Saucepan; 8-inch-square
pan, greased
Quantity: About 4 dozen pieces
Storing: Individually plastic-wrapped in
airtight container for 2 weeks

1 cup grated, peeled and cored Delicious apples	1 tablespoon rose extract
2 cups white sugar	1 cup finely chopped walnuts
2 tablespoons unflavored gelatin	confectioner's sugar
5 tablespoons cold water	

Place the grated apples and sugar in saucepan over
medium heat. Bring to a boil, stirring constantly;
boil for 1 minute. Turn heat low and simmer for 30
minutes.

Soak the gelatin in the water. When apple mixture has finished cooking, dissolve gelatin mixture
in it. Stirring constantly, add the extract and nuts.

Pour mixture into prepared pans. Cool at least 2
hours.

Cut into about 1-inch squares and roll each in
confectioner's sugar to coat. Let set at least 1 hour
before wrapping.

Never-Fail Chocolate Fudge

Utensils needed: Saucepan; Greased flat pan
or platter
Boiling time: 6 minutes
Quantity: Approximately 65 pieces
Storing: Individually plastic-wrapped in
airtight container for 1 week

1 6-ounce package chocolate bits	1 cup nut pieces
1 teaspoon pure vanilla extract	10 large-size marshmallows
5 tablespoons unsalted butter	2 cups sugar
	1 small can evaporated milk

Place chocolate bits, vanilla, butter and nuts in a
large mixing bowl. Set aside.

Place marshmallows, sugar and evaporated milk
in saucepan. Bring to boil over medium heat, stirring constantly. Continue stirring and boil for exactly 6 minutes.

Remove from heat and pour marshmallow mixture over the chocolate mixture in bowl. Beat with
a spoon until creamy.

Pour onto prepared pan or platter and cool
slightly before cutting into squares.

Turtles

Utensils needed: Double boiler; Cookie sheets, buttered
Quantity: About 4 dozen
Storing: Individually plastic-wrapped in airtight container for 2 weeks

1 pound vanilla caramels
8 teaspoons water
1 teaspoon pure vanilla extract

12 ounces semisweet chocolate
1½ cups pecan halves

Melt caramels with water and vanilla over boiling water in double boiler. Cool slightly. Separately, melt chocolate and set aside in a warm place.

Place 4 pecan halves on buttered cookie sheet. Spoon about 1 teaspoon of caramel mixture in center of group of nuts, half covering each nut. Repeat until all nuts are used. Let stand about 10 minutes. Spread some melted chocolate over each candy. Let stand until set.

© M. Weiss/FPG International

Bourbon Balls

No cooking
Chilling time: 3 hours
Setting time: 24 hours
Utensils needed: Mixing bowl
Quantity: About 6–7 dozen
Storing: Airtight container for 3 weeks

2½ cups crushed vanilla wafers
1 cup confectioner's sugar
2 tablespoons cocoa powder

1 cup finely chopped macadamia nuts
¼ cup bourbon (or rum)
3 tablespoons white corn syrup confectioner's sugar

Place all ingredients in a mixing bowl. Knead together with your hands until well-blended.

Roll dough into 1-inch balls. Roll each ball in confectioner's sugar until well-coated.

Chill at least 3 hours before storing. Let set at least 24 hours before serving.

© Jeanetta Ho

Almond Mounds

Preheat oven to: 350 degrees
Utensils needed: Double boiler; Baking sheet
Quantity: About 2 dozen pieces
Storing: Airtight container for 10 days

1¼ cups slivered
 blanched almonds
1 14-ounce can
 sweetened
 condensed milk

1 6-ounce package
 semisweet chocolate
 bits
1 teaspoon orange
 extract
1 teaspoon grated
 fresh orange rind

Place almond slivers on a baking sheet in a 350-degree oven and toast for about 7 minutes. Set aside.

Place chocolate bits and condensed milk in top of double boiler over very hot water (do not boil). Cook, stirring occasionally, for about 20 minutes or until quite thick. Remove from heat. Stir in extract, rind and toasted almond slivers, blending together until well-mixed.

Drop by the teaspoon onto waxed paper or foil. Refrigerate until well-set.

Truffles

Utensils needed: Double boiler; 8-inch-square
 pan, lined with foil
Cooling time: 2 hours
Quantity: About 2 pounds
Storing: Layers in airtight container for 2
 weeks

1 large egg white
2 tablespoons brandy
2 tablespoons cocoa
 powder
1½ cups sifted
 confectioner's
 sugar
1½ cups finely
 ground almonds
1½ cups grated
 unsweetened
 chocolate

1 tablespoon
 unsalted butter
¾ cup sweetened
 condensed milk

Place the egg white, brandy, cocoa, sifted sugar and almonds in a small bowl. Stir ingredients; then knead together by hand. Form in a layer in the bottom of the prepared pan.

Place the grated chocolate in top of double boiler over hot, but not boiling, water. Melt, stirring occasionally. Add the milk and butter and continue cooking until mixture thickens, about 7 minutes. Pour chocolate mixture over nut mixture in pan. Spread to make an even layer.

Cool at least 2 hours. When cool, cut into approximately 1-inch squares. Let set before storing.

Thermometer Candy

Holiday Fruit Candy

*Utensils needed: Saucepan; Candy ther-
mometer; 9-inch loaf pan, greased*
Standing time: 12 hours
Quantity: 4½ pounds
*Storing: Individually plastic-wrapped in
airtight container for 2 weeks*

3 cups sugar	½ pound walnut
1 cup light corn	halves
syrup	½ pound almonds
1½ cups heavy cream	½ pound whole
1 teaspoon pure	candied cherries
vanilla extract	½ cup diced candied
½ pound pecan	pineapple
halves	

Mix sugar, corn syrup and heavy cream in saucepan. Bring to boil and cook without stirring to 236
degrees on candy thermometer. Remove from heat
and let stand 5 minutes.

Add vanilla and beat until slightly thickened.
Add nuts and fruits and stir until well-mixed and
thick.

Pack into prepared pan and let stand overnight
or until firm. Turn out of pan and cut into thick
slices. Cut each slice into fingers.

Jumbles

*Utensils needed: Saucepan; Candy ther-
mometer*
Setting time: 2 hours
Quantity: About 2½ dozen
Storing: Airtight container for 10 days

½ cup white sugar	1¼ cups chopped
1 cup tightly packed	nuts (any kind will
light-brown sugar	do)
¼ cup white corn	½ cup flaked coconut
syrup	1½ teaspoons maple
½ cup evaporated	flavoring
milk	
2 tablespoons	
softened unsalted	
butter	

Place sugars, syrup and milk in saucepan over
medium heat. Cook, stirring constantly, until mixture reaches the soft-ball stage (240 degrees on
candy thermometer).

Remove from heat. Using a wooden spoon, immediately beat in the butter, nuts, coconut and
flavoring. Working quickly, drop mixture by the
teaspoonful onto waxed paper or foil. Cool.

Let set at least 2 hours before storing.

Peanut Brittle

Utensils needed: Saucepan; Candy thermometer; 2 cookie pans, greased
Setting time: 2 hours
Quantity: About 4 pounds
Storing: Airtight container in layers for 3 weeks

1 cup white corn
  syrup
4 cups sugar
5 cups unsalted
  roasted peanuts (or
  other nuts)
1½ tablespoons
  unsalted butter
2½ teaspoons baking
  soda

Place the syrup and sugar in a saucepan over medium heat. Cook, stirring constantly, until sugar dissolves. Place candy thermometer in pan and continue cooking, without stirring, until syrup reaches soft-ball stage (240 degrees on candy thermometer). Immediately add nuts. Cook, stirring occasionally, until syrup reaches hard-crack stage (300 degrees on candy thermometer).

Remove from heat. Immediately add butter and baking soda, stirring until well blended. Mixture will foam. Quickly pour mixture into prepared pans.

Cool at least 2 hours. Use a knife to break candy into serving pieces. Then let candy set about another 2 hours before storing.

Simple Pralines

Utensils needed: Saucepan; Candy thermometer
Quantity: About 1 dozen
Storing: Layers in airtight container for 10 days

2 cups tightly packed light-brown sugar	1 teaspoon pure vanilla extract
1 cup light cream	2½ cups pecan halves

Place sugar and cream in saucepan over medium heat. Cook, stirring constantly, until sugar dissolves. Continue cooking, without stirring, until

mixture reaches soft-ball stage (240 degrees on candy thermometer).

Remove from heat. Stir in vanilla. Beat until mixture begins to sugar. Immediately add pecans.

Drop on waxed paper into about 2½-inch patties. Cool before storing.

and creamy and holds its shape. Add flavoring and nuts (if desired).

Spread in prepared pan or drop by the teaspoonful onto waxed paper. If placed in pan, let set at least 2 hours before cutting into squares.

NOTE: If desired, you can add ½ cup chocolate bits or ½ cup candied fruit to this recipe in place of the nuts.

Divinity

Utensils needed: Saucepan; Candy thermometer; Electric mixer; 9-inch-square pan, greased
Setting time: 2 hours
Quantity: About 1¾ pounds
Storing: Layers in tightly covered container for 1 week

3 cups sugar (white or light-brown)	1 teaspoon pure vanilla extract (or other flavoring)
½ cup white corn syrup	1 cup chopped nuts (optional)
⅔ cup warm water	
2 large egg whites	

Place sugar, syrup and water in saucepan over medium heat. Cook, stirring constantly, until sugar dissolves. Continue cooking, without stirring, until mixture reaches the firm-ball stage (248 degrees on candy thermometer).

Stiffly beat the egg whites. Very slowly, pour about half the syrup mixture over them, mixing constantly.

Continue cooking the other half of the syrup mixture until it reaches the soft-crack stage (270 degrees on candy thermometer). Add it slowly to the egg white–syrup mixture. Beat until it is thick

Brandy Almond Chews

Utensils needed: Saucepan; Candy thermometer; 9-inch-square pan, greased
Boiling time: 5 minutes
Quantity: About 5 dozen
Storing: Individually plastic-wrapped in airtight container for 10 days

1 cup superfine sugar	4 squares unsweetened chocolate
1 cup dark corn syrup	2 teaspoons brandy
½ cup water	1 cup unblanched toasted whole almonds
½ cup light cream	
4 teaspoons unsalted butter	

In saucepan mix sugar, corn syrup, water and light cream. Bring to boil and boil 5 minutes. Add the butter and cook gently, stirring occasionally, to 230 degrees on candy thermometer. Add chocolate, bring to boil again and cook, stirring occasionally, until candy thermometer registers 240 degrees. Remove from heat and stir in brandy. Pour into greased pan. Cool completely.

Popcorn Balls

Utensils needed: Saucepan; Candy thermometer; Large bowl, greased
Quantity: About 1 dozen medium balls
Storing: Each ball in tightly closed plastic wrap, in dry place up to 2 weeks

1 cup sugar	*food coloring*
⅓ cup white corn syrup	*(optional)*
1 cup water	*3 quarts popped corn*
1 teaspoon lemon extract	*margarine to grease hands*

Place sugar, syrup and water in saucepan over medium heat. Cook, stirring frequently, to the soft-crack stage (280 degrees on candy thermometer). Remove from heat. Immediately add extract and

© M. Greenberg/FPG International

food coloring (if desired). Mix well.

Quickly pour syrup over popped corn in a large greased bowl. Stir with a fork, making sure most pieces of corn are coated. Working fast, grease your hands and scoop up enough coated corn to make a medium-sized ball. Shape and place on waxed paper to cool. This must be done very quickly or the syrup will cool and it will be impossible to form balls. Cool thoroughly before storing.

Popcorn balls in red and green make marvelous Christmas-tree ornaments. String them with a needle and heavy thread.

Sesame Butter Toffee

Utensils needed: Saucepan; Candy thermometer; Cookie sheet, greased
Preheat oven to: 350 degrees, to toast sesame seeds
Quantity: 1½ pounds
Storing: Layers in tightly covered container, for 2 weeks

1 cup toasted sesame seeds	*2 tablespoons water*
1 cup melted unsalted butter	*¾ teaspoon baking soda*
1 cup sugar	*3 squares semisweet chocolate, grated*
⅓ cup tightly packed light-brown sugar	

To toast sesame seeds: Place on cookie sheet and bake at 350 degrees for about 15 minutes or until golden brown.

Sprinkle about half the toasted seeds over the bottom of prepared pan. Set other half aside.

Place the melted butter, sugars and water in

saucepan. Bring to a boil, stirring constantly. Cook, stirring frequently, to soft-crack state (290 degrees on candy thermometer). Remove from heat. Immediately stir in baking soda and pour into prepared pan. Cool about 5 minutes.

Sprinkle grated chocolate over top of candy, smoothing as you go. Top with remaining toasted seeds. If necessary, press seeds gently into chocolate. Cool at least 2 hours. Break into serving pieces.

Penuche

Utensils needed: Saucepan; Candy thermometer; 8-inch-square pan, generously greased
Setting time: 1 hour
Quantity: 2½ pounds
Storing: Layers in airtight container for 10 days

2 cups tightly packed
  light-brown sugar
1 cup white sugar
1 tablespoon white
  corn syrup
¾ cup milk

1 tablespoon
  unsalted butter
1 teaspoon pure
  vanilla extract
1½ cups chopped
  walnuts

Place sugars, syrup, milk and butter in saucepan over medium heat. Cook, stirring constantly, until sugar dissolves. Continue cooking, without stirring, until mixture reaches soft-ball stage (240 degrees on candy thermometer).

Remove from heat. Stir in vanilla and nuts. Beat until mixture is very thick and has begun to lose its gloss. Pour into prepared pan. Let cool at least 1 hour. Cut into approximately 1-inch squares.

Chocolate Nut Caramels

Utensils needed: Saucepan; Candy thermometer; 8-inch-square pan, greased
Quantity: 1 pound
Storing: Individually plastic-wrapped in airtight container for 2 weeks

1 15-ounce can
  sweetened
  condensed milk
1 cup light corn
  syrup
1 tablespoon
  unsalted butter
2 squares
  unsweetened
  chocolate
1 teaspoon pure
  vanilla extract
¼ teaspoon rum
  extract
⅔ cup finely chopped
  macadamia nuts

Mix ⅓ cup condensed milk and corn syrup and butter. Cook over medium heat, stirring constantly, to 235 degrees on candy thermometer. Stir in remaining milk, keeping mixture boiling. Add chocolate, one square at a time. Cook until mixture again reaches 235 degrees on candy thermometer.

Remove from heat and stir in vanilla and rum extracts.

Sprinkle half of nuts in prepared pan and pour in caramel mixture. Sprinkle with remaining nuts and cool thoroughly. Cut into small squares.

© Steven Mark Needham/Envision

Coffee-Bean Fudge

Utensils needed: *Saucepan; Candy ther-mometer; 8-inch-square pan, buttered*
Quantity: *1 ½ pounds*
Storing: *Individually plastic-wrapped in airtight container for 1 week*

3 cups sugar	⅛ teaspoon salt
2 tablespoons instant espresso coffee powder	1 cup milk
	3 tablespoons unsalted butter
½ cup light cream	½ teaspoon rum extract
2 tablespoons light corn syrup	coffee beans

Mix sugar, coffee powder, salt, light cream, corn syrup and milk in a saucepan. Bring mixture to boil, stirring constantly. Continue cooking without stirring to 234 degrees on candy thermometer.

Remove from heat. Add butter and rum extract, but do not stir.

Cool to lukewarm. Then beat until mixture begins to thicken and loses its gloss.

Spread in prepared pan. While still warm, mark in squares and press a coffee bean into center of each square. When cold, cut into pieces.

Chocolate Walnut Crunch

Utensils needed: *Saucepan; Candy ther-mometer; Cookie sheet, greased*
Quantity: *2 pounds*
Cooking time: *45 minutes*
Storing: *Individually plastic-wrapped in airtight container for 1 week*

2 cups unsalted butter	2 cups coarsely chopped walnuts
2 cups sugar	6 ounces semisweet chocolate
¼ cup water	
2 tablespoons light corn syrup	½ cup finely chopped walnuts

Melt butter over low heat. Add sugar and stir until sugar is melted. Add water and corn syrup. Continue cooking without stirring until mixture reaches 290 degrees on candy thermometer.

Remove from heat and stir in coarsely chopped walnuts. Spread in prepared pan and let stand until firm.

Melt chocolate over hot water and spread melted chocolate evenly on candy. Sprinkle with finely chopped walnuts. Let stand until firm and break into pieces.

 Nut Candies

Sour-Cream Candied Nuts

Utensils needed: Saucepan; Candy thermometer
Quantity: About 1 pound
Storing: Individually plastic-wrapped in airtight container for 2 weeks

1½ cups sugar
½ cup sour cream
1 teaspoon pure
   vanilla extract

2½ cups walnut
   halves

Mix sugar and sour cream in saucepan. Bring to a boil and cook, stirring, until 236 degrees is reached on candy thermometer.

Remove from heat and add vanilla. Beat until mixture thickens and loses its gloss. Add nuts and stir to coat them on all sides. Put on greased cookie sheet and separate nuts.

Orange Walnuts

Utensils needed: Saucepan; Candy thermometer
Quantity: 2½ cups
Storing: Airtight container for 2 weeks

© Tom Tracy/FPG International

¼ cup lukewarm
   water
3½ tablespoons fresh
   orange juice
1 tablespoon white
   corn syrup
1½ cups sugar

¼ cup grated fresh
   orange juice
1 teaspoon grated
   fresh lemon rind
2½ cups walnut
   halves

Place water, orange juice, syrup and sugar in saucepan over medium heat. Cook, stirring constantly, until mixture begins to boil. Continue to cook, without stirring, until mixture reaches the soft-ball stage (240 degrees on candy thermometer).

Remove from heat. Immediately add the grated rinds and walnut halves. Stir gently until mixture is creamy and nuts are well-coated. Turn out onto a large sheet of waxed paper or foil. Separate nuts with 2 forks. Cool thoroughly before storing.

Glazed Nuts

Utensils needed: Saucepan; Candy thermometer
Quantity: 1 pound
Storing: Airtight container up to 2 weeks

1½ cups sugar
½ cup honey
½ cup water
½ teaspoon pure vanilla extract

1 pound mixed unsalted nuts (or any one kind of nut)

Mix sugar, honey and water in a saucepan. Bring to boil and cook without stirring to 242 degrees on a candy thermometer.

Remove from heat and stir in nuts and vanilla. Let cool slightly. Stir again until creamy. Then place on waxed paper and separate nuts with 2 forks.

Spiced Mixed Nuts

Preheat oven to: 350 degrees
Utensils needed: Cookie sheet
Baking time: 15 minutes
Quantity: 2½ cups
Storing: Airtight container for 4 weeks

¼ cup vegetable oil
2 cups sifted confectioner's sugar

1 large egg white, slightly beaten
½ teaspoon ground nutmeg

½ teaspoon ground cinnamon
1½ teaspoons brandy

1½ cups unsalted mixed nuts

Cream together all ingredients except nuts. Put nuts on cookie sheet and heat in 350-degree oven for 15 minutes. Add to creamed spice-oil mixture and stir well to coat each nut. Spread out on cooled cookie sheet or platter to dry.

Sugared Nuts

Utensils needed: Saucepan; Candy thermometer; Pie pan
Quantity: 1½ pounds
Storing: Airtight container for 2 weeks

1 cup sugar
2 cups maple syrup
1½ pounds walnut or pecan halves (or any kind of nuts)

granulated sugar for coating
confectioner's sugar for dusting

Combine 1 cup sugar and maple syrup in saucepan. Bring to a boil and boil gently to 230 degrees on candy thermometer. Remove from heat and cool slightly.

Spread a layer of nuts in bottom of pie pan. Dribble syrup over nuts, stirring with a metal spoon. Add more nuts and repeat process until all nuts are coated with syrup.

Place granulated sugar on large pan or platter. With a slotted spoon, lift nuts out of the syrup. Place on sugar and stir until well-coated. Dust with confectioner's sugar to taste. Dry thoroughly before storing.

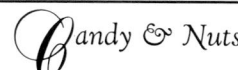

Candy & Nuts

Rasberry-Peach Jam

Jellies, Marmalades, Jams & Conserves

© T. Lindley/FPG International

Homemade jellies, jams, marmalades and conserves are easy to make. In almost all of the recipes that follow we have used commercial fruit pectin. This ensures that your product will turn out correctly. For any recipe using commercial pectin, you should always use fully ripe fruit.

For making the recipes in this chapter, the following utensils are required:

Large *heavy* kettle for cooking fruit.

Large kettle or pot for boiling jars and covers; or a large roasting pan.

One-pound empty coffee can for melting paraffin.

Wire rack for cooling jars.

Large metal spoon for skimming.

Tongs for lifting jars out of sterlizing bath.

Large wooden spoon for stirring.

You do not have to use proper jelly or jam jars. Any mayonnaise, instant-coffee, baby-food or spaghetti sauce jars you have in your cupboard will do as well. Be sure that they are thoroughly scoured and rinsed and are odorless before use.

All of the following recipes are to be cooked in an uncovered kettle.

If you do purchase jars, we find that the jelly jars with loose-fitting metal lids are best. These hold about 8 ounces. There are also canning jars in various sizes. We prefer the type with a two-part cover: an inner rib lined with rubber and an outer cap that screws on over it. We think that the 8-ounce size is best for this type of jar also. It is not necessary to seal these with paraffin before putting the lids on. Sterilize lids and jars together, and screw on tops immediately after filling.

Paraffin for sealing jars can be bought in almost any hardware store or supermarket. *Always* place paraffin in a separate container, preferably a coffee can, and *set it in a pan filled with water.* Heat the water over medium heat, being careful that it does not bubble over into the paraffin. It is important to remember *never to melt paraffin over direct heat; it is highly flammable.* If paraffin hardens before you are ready to use it, just reheat it to melt again.

Jars and lids to be sterilized must first be washed and rinsed. Then place them in a large kettle (or roasting pan) with enough water to cover. Bring them to a boil slowly and simmer for about 20 minutes, uncovered. When jam is ready, remove jars from water with a pair of tongs and place on wire racks. *Immediately* fill jars with *hot* jam to within ½ inch of the top. If jelly jars are used, seal immediately with ⅛-inch layer of melted paraffin. When paraffin has hardened completely, cover with an additional ⅛-inch layer of melted paraffin. After this layer hardens completely, cover with lids. If you do not

have jar lids, a double piece of aluminum foil held by a rubber band is fine.

If you are using canning jars with screw-top covers, tighten again after jars have cooled completely.

You can decorate just the lid or the entire jar. Lids may be covered with foil, felt, crepe paper or adhesive-backed decorating paper. Bows or small ornaments may be attached with double-faced masking tape. A very simple method of decoration is to buy notary seals and cover the tops with them.

For those of you with a bit more patience, you can wind raffia or colored yarn around the tops. To do this, thinly spread lids with white glue. Start at the edge of the rim and carefully wind raffia or yarn around, keeping rows very close together. Reapply a small amount of glue if necessary. Apply small amount of glue to the end of the raffia or yarn and tuck it under, using a clean toothpick.

You can also decorate tops simply by gluing peppercorns, popcorn (unpopped), beans, poppy seeds and cloves in a pattern on jar lids. You do not have to use all of these, but a combination is most attractive. The lids should then be sprayed with clear plastic to preserve the design.

The jars themselves may be decorated with china markers in whatever design you wish. You may also make stripes with colored plastic tape or cut designs

© Judd Pilossof

out of self-adhesive plastic. The decorated jars can then be placed in homemade drawstring bags or small foil or gift bags.

Homemade jellies, jams, marmalades and conserves store indefinitely in the pantry exactly like store-bought ones.

Jellies

Rosé-Wine Jelly

Utensils needed: Kettle
Quantity: About 4 4-ounce jars

3 cups rosé wine
¾ cup water
⅛ teaspoon fresh
  lemon juice
2 tablespoons
  powdered light
  fruit pectin

3½ cups sugar
5 or more whole
  cloves per jar
fresh mint leaves
  (optional)

Place wine, lemon juice and powdered pectin in kettle over high heat. Cook, stirring constantly, to the simmering point. Immediately add sugar. Cook, stirring constantly, until jelly comes to a full, rolling boil. Quickly remove from heat and skim off foam with a metal spoon.

Place at least five cloves in the bottom of each hot, sterilized jar. Pour in jelly. If desired, you can at this point also add a mint leaf. Seal at once (see page 74).

Let jelly set about 1 hour; then turn jars upside down and shake gently to distribute cloves.

NOTE: When giving as a gift, let recipient know that this jelly is used primarily as a glaze for or accompaniment to meats.

Marjoram or Sage Jelly

Utensils needed: Kettle; Cheesecloth
Standing time: 20 minutes
Quantity: 4 4-ounce jars

1 cup boiling water
2 tablespoons minced
  fresh marjoram or
  sage
⅓ cup fresh lemon
  juice
3 cups sugar

1 pouch liquid fruit
  pectin
2 to 3 drops food
  coloring—red for
  marjoram, green
  for sage

Pour boiling water over marjoram or sage. Cover and let stand 20 minutes. Strain through cheesecloth and add enough water to make 1 cup. Strain lemon juice through cheesecloth. Place herb infusion and lemon juice in kettle over high heat and add sugar. Stir well and bring to boil. Add pectin and stir vigorously. Add food coloring and continue stirring until mixture comes to full, rolling boil. Boil hard for exactly ½ minute. Remove from heat and skim with metal spoon. Pour at once into hot, sterilized jars and seal with paraffin.

NOTE: These jellies are served primarily with meats or poultry. They are both good with chicken, veal, ham or roast beef.

Cranberry-Claret Jelly

Utensils needed: Double boiler
Quantity: 4 4-ounce jars

3½ cups sugar
1 cup unsweetened
  cranberry juice

1 cup claret wine
1 pouch liquid fruit
  pectin

Put sugar, cranberry juice and wine in top of double boiler and mix well. Place over rapidly boiling water and stir until sugar is dissolved, about 2 minutes. Remove from heat and stir in pectin. Skim off foam and pour into sterilized jars. Seal at once (see page 74).

© E. Cooper/FPG International

Spicy Grape Jelly

Utensils needed: Kettle; Cheesecloth bag
Boiling time: 1 minute
Quantity: About 5 4-ounce jars

2 cups unsweetened
  grape juice
2 cups cold water
2 drops white
  vinegar
4 whole allspice

3 large cinnamon
  sticks, broken
15 whole cloves
1 box powdered light
  fruit pectin
3½ cups sugar

Place juice and water in kettle. Stir and add vinegar. Tie all spices together in cheesecloth bag and add to juice mixture. Stir in powdered pectin.

Place kettle over high heat. Stirring frequently, bring to a full, rolling boil and immediately add sugar. Bring again to a full, rolling boil. Stir and boil for 1 minute. Remove from heat and skim off foam with a metal spoon. Remove spice bag and pour jelly into hot, sterilized jars. Seal at once (see page 74).

NOTE: When giving this jelly as a gift, let recipient know that although it is tasty on toast, it is particularly good with meats or as a glaze.

Jams

Raspberry-Peach Jam

Utensils needed: Kettle
Quantity: Approximately 6 8-ounce jars

3 cups crushed red
raspberry
3 cups peeled, pitted
and chopped ripe
peaches

2 tablespoons fresh
lemon juice
1 box light fruit
pectin
3½ cups sugar

Place fruit, lemon peel, lemon rind and ginger root in kettle over high heat. Stir in ½ cup sugar and light fruit pectin.

Bring to a full, rolling boil over high heat and add remaining sugar.

Immediately bring to a full, rolling boil again and, stirring constantly, boil for 1 minute.

Remove from heat and stir in crystallized ginger, if used. Ladle into hot, sterilized jars and seal at once (see page 74).

© Brian Leatart

Lemon-Ginger-Pear Jam

Utensils needed: Kettle
Quantity: 8 8-ounce jars

5 cups peeled, cored
and chopped
Bartlett pears
¼ cup fresh lemon
juice
1 tablespoon grated
fresh lemon rind
2 tablespoons grated
fresh ginger root

3½ cups sugar
1 box powdered light
fruit pectin
¼ cup minced
crystallized ginger
(optional)

Place fruit and lemon juice in kettle over high heat. Stir in light fruit pectin and ¼ cup sugar.

Bring to a full, rolling boil over high heat and add remaining sugar.

Immediately bring to a full, rolling boil again and, stirring constantly, boil for 1 minute.

Remove from heat and skim off any foam. Ladle into hot, sterilized jars and seal at once (see page 74).

Sour-Cherry Jam

Utensils needed: Kettle
Quantity: Approximately 11 8-ounce jars

5 cups fully ripe
  stemmed, pitted
  and chopped sour
  cherries
3¼ cups sugar
1 box powdered light

fruit pectin
¼–½ teaspoon
  almond extract
1 cup finely chopped
  almonds

Place cherries into kettle. Add ¼ cup sugar and pectin.

Bring to a full, rolling boil over high heat and add remaining sugar.

Remove from heat and immediately stir in almond extract and almonds. Skim foam off the top with a metal spoon, stirring and skimming for 5 minutes.

Immediately bring to a full, rolling boil again and, stirring constantly, boil for 1 minute.

Ladle into hot, sterilized jars and seal at once (see page 74).

Mango-Lime Jam

Utensils needed: Kettle
Quantity: 8 8-ounce jars

6 cups peeled, pitted
  and crushed
  mango
⅓ cup fresh lime juice

4 cups sugar
1 box powdered light
  fruit pectin

Place mango and lime juice in kettle over high heat. Stir in ½ cup sugar and light fruit pectin.

Bring to a full, rolling boil over high heat and add remaining sugar.

Immediately bring to a full, rolling boil again and, stirring constantly, boil for 1 minute.

Remove from heat and ladle into hot, sterilized jars and seal at once (see page 74).

Marmalades

Honey-Grapefruit Marmalade

Utensils needed: Food processor; Kettle
Preparation time: Allow 4 days
Quantity: About 8 8-ounce jars

1 large clean-skinned grapefruit	*half as much sugar as cooked fruit*
1 large lemon	*half as much honey*
water	*as cooked fruit*

Peel the grapefruit and lemon, cutting only the colored part of the rind. Slice the peel into very thin strips.

Seed the pulp. Chop the pulp, including the white of the rind, in the food processor using the metal blade. Do not lose juice.

Place the rind and pulp in kettle, measuring as you go. For each cup fruit, add 3 cups cold water. Let sit, tightly covered for 24 hours.

Place over medium heat and cook, stirring frequently, until mixture comes to a boil. Boil for 15 minutes. Cover and let stand 24 hours.

Again, cook as above. Cover and let stand another 24 hours.

Remeasure mixture. Add half as much sugar and half as much honey. Cook, stirring frequently, until mixture is thick and clear and has begun to jell. Pour into hot, sterilized jars and seal at once (see page 74).

Lime Marmalade

Utensils needed: Food processor; Kettle
Preparation time: Allow 3 days
Quantity: About 5 8-ounce jars

9 large limes	*water*
1 large lemon	*sugar*

Wash fruit. Cut in half and seed. Chop in food processor using the metal blade. Do not lose juice.

Measure the ground fruit. To each cup fruit add 3 cups water. Mix thoroughly. Place in kettle and let stand 24 hours, covered, in a cool place. Do not refrigerate.

Place over medium heat and cook, stirring constantly, until mixture comes to a boil. Boil, without stirring, for 10 minutes. Again, set aside as above.

Measure the cooked fruit. Add 1 cup more sugar than fruit. Cook over medium heat, stirring frequently, for about 30 minutes, or until marmalade begins to jell. Pour immediately into hot, sterilized jars and seal at once (see page 74).

Apricot-Orange-Pineapple Marmalade

Utensils needed: Food processor; Kettle
Quantity: About 10 8-ounce jars

1 large fresh
   pineapple
3 pounds fresh
   apricots
1 large clear-skinned
   orange

½ cup sugar to each
   cup fruit
1 tablespoon grated
   fresh ginger

Peel and core pineapple. Pit and quarter apricots. Seed and chop orange. Do not lose juice from fruits. Chop all fruit together in food processor using the metal blade.

Measure fruit as you pour it into heavy kettle. Add ½ cup sugar for each cup fruit. Stir in the ginger.

Cook over medium heat for about 45 minutes or until marmalade is thick and clear. Pour into hot, sterilized jars and seal at once (see page 74).

Conserves

Apricot-Clementine Conserve

Utensils needed: Food processor; Kettle
Quantity: About 5 8-ounce jars

1 pound dried
   apricots
1 quart cold water
3 clementines (or
   tangerines)
½ cup fresh orange
   juice

juice of 1 lemon
1 cup seedless white
   raisins
teaspoon Amaretto
2 cups sugar
2 cups chopped
   almonds

Place apricots in kettle and cover with 1 quart cold water. Cover tightly and let stand 24 hours.

Seed and chop the clementines in the food processor using the metal blade. Add the chopped clementines, juices, raisins, and sugar to the apricots and water. Cook over medium heat, stirring constantly, until mixture comes to the boiling point. Boil, stirring occasionally, until conserve is thick and clear. Quickly stir in Amaretto and chopped nuts.

Remove from heat and pour into hot, sterilized jars. Seal at once (see page 74).

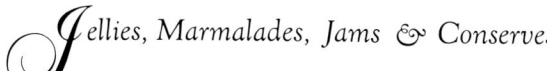

Cranberry Conserve

Utensils needed: Kettle
Cooking time: About 15 minutes
Quantity: 4 8-ounce jars

2 cups water	½ cup broken
2 cups sugar	macadamia nuts
1½ pounds	¼ cup chopped
cranberries	crystallized ginger
grated rind of 1	
orange	

Place water and sugar in kettle and stir until sugar is dissolved. Boil for 5 minutes, then add cranberries. Simmer until the skins pop on berries and mixture is thick and clear. This should take about 10 minutes.

Add grated orange rind, nuts and ginger. Immediately pour into hot, sterilized jars and seal at once (see page 74).

¼ teaspoon ground cloves	1½ cups chopped unsalted mixed
1 teaspoon ground cinnamon	peanuts
	dash Tabasco

Place diced rhubarb in kettle.

Seed and juice the lemon, lime and oranges. Remove the pulp and discard it. Slice the skin very fine and add the juice and rind to the rhubarb. Stir in the raisins, jalapeño, cloves, cinnamon and sugar.

Cook over medium heat, stirring constantly, until sugar is dissolved. Bring to a boil. Boil gently, without stirring, about 45 minutes, or until mixture is thick and clear.

Remove from heat. Stir in chopped nuts and Tabasco. Pour into hot, sterilized jars. Seal at once (see page 74).

Spicy Rhubarb Conserve

Utensils needed: Kettle
Cooking time: 45 minutes to 1 hour
Quantity: About 6 8-ounce jars

4 cups diced rhubarb	1 cup seedless raisins
1 lemon	½ seeded and minced
1 lime	jalapeño pepper
2 oranges	4 cups sugar

Tutti-Frutti

*Utensils needed: Stone crock—capacity at
 least 8 quarts
No cooking
Preparation time: Allow 5 to 6 weeks
Quantity: About 14 8-ounce jars*

1 pound peaches	*1 pound black figs*
1 pound plums	*1 pound green*
1 pound Seckel pears	*seedless grapes*
1 pound nectarines	*1 pound black grapes*
1 pound red seedless	*approximately 5*
grapes	*pounds sugar*

Prick the peaches, plums, pears and nectarines
with a fork. Pack all the fruit into the crock in
layers, covering each fruit layer with sugar. Cover
and let stand in a cool place, stirring up every three
days.

After one week, when the fruit floats, press
down with a plate and nonmetal weight and cover
with waxed paper. Let fruit stand, stirring occasionally, until fermentation is complete—about one
month or so.

When fermentation is complete, pack into sterilized jars. Seal and store in cool place or refrigerator
(see page 74).

NOTE: Tutti-Frutti may be used as a dessert, or the
fruit may be glazed in roasting-pan juices and
served with game, poultry or pork. We suggest that
you give these serving directions along with your
gift.

Jack Daniel's Sauce

❧❧❧

Syrups, Sauces and Flavors

© David Spindel/FPG International

Syrups, sauces and flavors are among the easiest of gifts in this book.

Syrups can be used to make refreshing summer drinks or as an additive to punches. They are wonderful on waffles, pancakes, French toast or ice cream.

Three different dessert sauces, we think, make a lovely house gift. They can be made quickly and are always handy. They enable the recipient to turn plain cake or ice cream into a festive treat.

You can give the flavored or spiced sugar with a tin of imported cocoa or a fine tea. The flavored coconut is a great extra with dessert sauces or for someone who likes to bake.

We recommend using 12-ounce bottles (such as those from ketchup, carbonated beverages or maple syrup) for our syrups. You can also purchase bottles through gourmet stores or mail-order catalogs. For most of the sauces, we recommend the use of smaller (4-ounce) jars. The flavors do best in a small mustard-type jar. Empty spice jars are also good for the flavors, but do be sure that they are odorless before use. All bottles and jars used must have tight-fitting caps.

For those recipes in this chapter whose containers need sterilizing and sealing, please follow the instructions given on page 74.

Syrups

Apricot Syrup

Utensils needed: Heavy saucepan; Electric blender
Cooking time: About 30 minutes
Quantity: 2 12-ounce bottles
Storing: Airtight containers, refrigerated, up to 6 weeks

1 11-ounce box dried apricots	½ cup light corn syrup
water	¼ cup fresh lemon juice
½ cup dark corn syrup	juice of 1 orange

Place apricots in saucepan and cover with water. Place over medium heat and simmer, covered, until tender—about 20 minutes. Drain, reserving about 1½ cups apricot cooking water.

Put the apricots in container of electric blender. Puree at high speed, adding apricot cooking liquid as necessary, for just a few seconds.

Pour pureed apricots back into the saucepan and add all remaining ingredients. Bring to a boil, lower heat and simmer for 10 minutes. If syrup is too thick add up to ½ cup cold water.

Pour into sterilized bottles. Cap tightly and refrigerate.

Apple Syrup

Utensils needed: Heavy saucepan
Cooking time: About 15 minutes
Quantity: 1 12-ounce bottle
Storing: Airtight container, refrigerated, up to 6 weeks

1 cup unsweetened apple juice	¼ cup calvados
1 cup sugar	1 cinnamon stick

Combine all ingredients in saucepan over medium heat. Bring to a boil, stirring constantly, and boil for about 15 minutes or until slightly thickened. Remove from heat and pour, including the cinnamon stick, into sterilized 12-ounce bottle. Cap tightly and refrigerate.

Grape Syrup

Utensils needed: Heavy saucepan
Cooking time: About 10 minutes
Quantity: 1 12-ounce bottle
Storing: Airtight container, refrigerated, up
to 6 weeks

2 cups unsweetened white grape juice	1 tablespoon fresh lemon juice
1½ cups sugar	

Combine grape juice and sugar in saucepan. Bring to a boil over medium heat, stirring constantly.

Boil for 5 minutes, then remove from heat and skim off foam with a metal spoon. Stir in lemon juice.

Pour into sterilized 12-ounce bottle. Cap tightly and refrigerate.

Cinnamon Syrup

Utensils needed: Heavy saucepan
Cooking time: About 45 minutes
Quantity: 1 12-ounce bottle
Storing: Airtight container, refrigerated, up
to 6 weeks

4 cups unsweetened apple juice	½ cup red-hot cinnamon candies
½ cup light corn syrup	1 stick cinnamon

Combine all ingredients in saucepan over medium heat. Bring to a boil, lower heat and simmer until syrup is reduced to about 2½ cups; this should take about 45 minutes.

Pour, including the cinnamon stick, into sterilized 12-ounce bottle. Cap tightly and refrigerate.

© Steven Mark Needham/Envision

Framboise Syrup

Utensils needed: Heavy saucepan; Fine sieve
Cooking time: About 15 minutes
Quantity: 2 12-ounce bottles
Storing: Airtight container, refrigerated, up
to 6 weeks

3 10-ounce packages frozen strawberries or raspberries	¼ cup framboise
	2 cups sugar
	½ cup water

Combine berries, sugar and water in saucepan. Bring to a boil, over medium heat, stirring constantly.

Boil for about 15 minutes. When slightly thickened remove from heat and skim off foam with a metal spoon. Strain through sieve.

Pour into sterilized bottles. Cap tightly and refrigerate.

Sauces

Hot Fudge Sauce

Utensils needed: Heavy saucepan
Cooking time: About 15 minutes
Quantity: About 4 4-ounce jars
Storing: Airtight containers, refrigerated, up
to 1 month

½ cup cocoa powder
1 cup sugar
1 cup light corn
  syrup
½ cup light cream

3 tablespoons
  unsalted butter
1 teaspoon pure
  vanilla extract

Combine cocoa, sugar, syrup, cream and butter in saucepan. Cook over medium heat, stirring constantly, until mixture comes to full, rolling boil. Boil hard for 3 minutes, stirring occasionally.

Remove from heat and add vanilla.

Cool and pour into jars; cover and refrigerate.

Chocolate Sauce

Utensils needed: Heavy saucepan
Cooking time: About 12 minutes
Quantity: About 4 4-ounce jars
Storing: Airtight containers, refrigerated, up
to 3 weeks

½ cup cocoa powder
1 cup milk
⅔ cup sugar
1 teaspoon
  cornstarch
1 cup heavy cream

1 tablespoon
  unsalted butter
1 teaspoon pure
  vanilla extract

Place the cocoa and milk in saucepan. Stir to blend. Add the sugar, cornstarch and heavy cream.

Cook over medium heat, stirring constantly, until mixture is thick and smooth. Remove from heat.

© T. Lindley/FPG International

Add butter and vanilla. Beat for about 2 minutes.

Pour into jars, cover and refrigerate.

This sauce must be reheated for serving.

VARIATION:

For variety, you may add to the above ½ cup crushed peppermint-stick candy, ¾ cup chopped nuts, or any fruit or mint flavoring or liqueur in place of the vanilla.

Bittersweet Chocolate Sauce

Utensils needed: Heavy saucepan
Cooking time: About 15 minutes
Quantity: About 4 4-ounce jars
Storing: Airtight containers, refrigerated, up to 2 weeks

12 ounces semisweet chocolate	2 cups unsalted butter, chilled and cut in slices
¾ cup espresso or any other very strong coffee	1½ teaspoons pure vanilla extract

Place the chocolate and coffee in saucepan over moderate heat. Stir until chocolate is completely dissolved. Turn heat to low if chocolate starts to stick.

Remove from heat. Beat in the chilled butter, bit by bit, until you have used it all and it is completely absorbed. If mixture gets too cool to dissolve butter, return to heat—but do not stir in butter while mixture is on the heat. Stir in the vanilla.

Pour into jars, cover and refrigerate.

NOTE: This sauce may be used cold to frost a cake or warm on any desert. It is *very* thick and rich.

Macadamia-Nut Sauce

Utensils needed: Heavy saucepan
Cooking time: About 25 minutes
Quantity: About 6 4-ounce jars
Storing: Airtight containers, refrigerated, up to 2 weeks

1½ cups water	1 teaspoon grated fresh lemon rind
1 cup white sugar	
1 cup light-brown sugar	2 cups heavy cream
2 tablespoons fresh lemon juice	2½ cups chopped lightly toasted macadamia nuts

Place water, sugars, lemon juice and rind in heavy saucepan over low heat. Stir constantly until sugar is entirely dissolved. When sugar has dissolved, increase heat to medium high and boil until syrup is a very rich caramel color, about 15 minutes.

Remove from heat and slowly whisk in cream. (Sauce may bubble up if cream is poured too quickly.) Return to low heat and cook until sauce is slightly thickened, about 8 minutes. Immediately stir in nuts. Remove from heat and pour into jars. Cover and refrigerate.

Mocha Sauce

Utensils needed: Heavy saucepan
Cooking time: About 15 minutes
Quantity: About 4 4-ounce jars
Storing: Tightly covered, refrigerated, up to 2 weeks

⅓ cup unsalted butter	*3 tablespoons Grand Marnier*
1¼ cups chopped macadamia nuts	*2 tablespoons instant espresso coffee*
6 ounces semisweet chocolate	

Place butter in saucepan over very low heat. Stir until melted. Add the nuts and continue stirring until nuts begin to brown. Gradually add the chocolate, stirring constantly until it is melted.

Remove from heat. Stir in the Grand Marnier and the coffee. Blend well.

Pour into jars, cover and store in refrigerator.

This must be reheated for serving.

Peach Sauce

Utensils needed: Mixing bowl; Heavy saucepan
Cooking time: About 25 minutes
Quantity: About 8 4-ounce jars
Storing: Airtight containers, refrigerated, up to 2 weeks. May be frozen

8 medium-size fresh peaches	*¼ cup champagne or white wine*
1 cup sugar	*2 teaspoons pure vanilla extract*
1 cup fresh orange juice	

Peel, pit and crush peaches.

Combine fruit with sugar and orange juice in saucepan. Bring to a boil, stirring constantly, over high heat. Reduce heat to medium. Stir in champagne or wine and simmer, uncovered, for about 15 minutes, or until sauce begins to thicken.

Remove from heat. Stir in vanilla.

Pour into jars, cover and refrigerate.

Jack Daniel's Sauce

Utensils needed: Heavy saucepan
Cooking time: About 20 minutes
Quantity: Aboaut 4 4-ounce jars
Storing: Airtight containers, refrigerated, up
to 3 weeks

¾ cup water	*½ cup light-brown*
½ cup white sugar	*sugar*
1 tablespoon fresh	*1 cup heavy cream*
orange juice	*⅓ cup Jack Daniel's*
1 teaspoon fresh	*whiskey*
lemon juice	

Place water, sugars, orange juice and lemon juice in heavy saucepan over low heat. Stir constantly until sugars are dissolved. When sugars have dissolved, increase heat to medium high and boil until syrup is a rich caramel color, about 12 minutes.

Remove from heat and slowly whisk in cream (sauce may bubble up if cream is poured too quickly). Return to low heat and cook until sauce is slightly thickened, about 8 minutes. Immediately stir in Jack Daniel's.

Remove from heat and pour into jars. Cover and refrigerate.

Rum-Raisin Sauce

Utensils needed: Heavy saucepan
Cooking time: Raisins—1 hour; sauce—10
minutes

Quantity: About 8 4-ounce jars
Storing: Airtight containers, refrigerated, up
to 1 month

1 cup seedless white	*1 teaspoon fresh*
raisins	*lemon juice*
2 cups boiling water	*1 teaspoon grated*
1½ cups granulated	*fresh lemon rind*
sugar	*2 tablespoons*
2 teaspoons	*unsalted butter*
cornstarch	*¼ cup chopped*
½ cup rum	*macadamia nuts*

Place the raisins and boiling water in saucepan over medium heat. Simmer gently for about 1 hour.

Sift the sugar and cornstarch into the simmering raisins. Blend well and continue simmering for 10 more minutes.

Remove from heat and stir in remaining ingredients.

Pour into jars, cover and refrigerate.

This sauce must be reheated for use.

NOTE: Rum-Raisin Sauce is good on almost any fruit dessert or on plain cake. It can also be used as a meat glaze.

© Steven Mark Needham/Envision

Easy Orange Sauce

Utensils needed: Heavy saucepan
Cooking time: Approximately 5 minutes
Quantity: About 4 4-ounce jars
Storing: Airtight containers, refrigerated up
*   to 4 months*

3 cups imported bitter orange marmalade	1 tablespoon fresh lemon juice
½ cup Grand Marnier	1 teaspoon grated fresh lemon rind
¼ cup fresh orange juice	½ cup unsalted butter

Combine all ingredients in a heavy saucepan over medium heat. Bring to a boil and simmer, stirring constantly, for 10 minutes.

Remove from heat and pour into jars. Cover and refrigerate.

Butterscotch Sauce

Utensils needed: Heavy saucepan
Cooking time: About 20 minutes
Quantity: 4 to 5 4-ounce jars
Storing: Airtight containers, refrigerated, up
*   to 3 weeks*

1 cup dark corn syrup	½ cup granulated sugar

½ cup tightly packed light-brown sugar	2 tablespoons unsalted butter
¼ teaspoon salt	1 teaspoon pure vanilla extract
½ cup light cream	

Combine all ingredients except vanilla in saucepan. Bring to a full, rolling boil, stirring constantly, over medium heat. Boil 5 minutes, stirring occasionally.

Remove from heat and stir in vanilla.

Cool. Pour into jars, cover and refrigerate.

Butter-Rum Sauce

Utensils needed: Heavy saucepan; Candy
*   thermometer*
Cooking time: About 30 minutes
Quantity: About 5 4-ounce jars
Storing: Airtight containers, refrigerated, up
*   to 1 month*

1½ cups tightly packed dark-brown sugar	⅔ cup cold water
	¼ cup unsalted butter
⅔ cup light corn syrup	dash salt
	¼ cup Myer's rum

Combine all ingredients except rum in saucepan. Bring to a boil over medium heat. Cook, stirring frequently, until mixture reaches 230 degrees on candy thermometer.

Remove from heat and cool. When sauce is cool, stir in rum.

Pour into jars, cover and refrigerate.

This must be reheated for use.

NOTE: This is an excellent sauce for plain cakes.

Flavors

Flavored Coconut

Utensils needed: Mixing bowl
No cooking
Quantity: Each recipe yields 1 cup
Storing: Airtight container, refrigerated 6 months

ALMOND COCONUT

1 cup grated fresh coconut
2 teaspoons almond extract

Toss coconut and almond extract with fork to blend.

CRÈME DE CACAO OR CRÈME DE MENTHE COCONUT

2 tablespoons crème de cacao or crème de menthe

1 cup grated fresh coconut

Toss coconut and liqueur with fork to blend.

NOTE: These are good cake or ice cream toppings. Flavored coconut is also a great addition to a fruit salad.

GRENADINE COCONUT

1 cup grated fresh coconut
2 tablespoons grenadine

Toss coconut and grenadine lightly with fork to blend.

Assorted Spiced Fruits and Chutneys

Spiced Fruits & Chutneys

© Brian Leatart

Homemade spiced fruits and chutneys make excellent gifts, and the recipes included here are all quite easy.

Most of our recipes call for pint or half-pint jars. See page 74 for sterilizing and sealing instructions.

When giving spiced fruits or chutneys as a gift, we recommend that you include serving hints. For instance, Spiced Peaches are excellent with roast duck, and Spiced Crab Apples go particularly well with ham or pork. Although a chutney is usually thought of as an accompaniment to a curried dish, it is splendid with almost any kind of roast meat or poultry. Chutney is a particularly good way to add excitement to leftover cold meats—for instance, Apple Chutney with cold ham.

Spiced Fruits

Jubilee Pears

*Utensils needed: Saucepan; Covered storage
  container*
Preparation time: Allow 2 days
Quantity: 2 4-ounce jars

2 pounds firm ripe pears, peeled, cored and halved	1 cup sugar
	⅓ cup currant jelly
	1 stick cinnamon
2 cups water	⅓ cup burgundy
1 cup white wine	wine

Drain pears, reserving 1½ cups of the pear syrup, and set them aside.

Put the 1½ cups pear syrup, currant jelly and cinnamon stick in saucepan over medium heat.

© Myrleen Ferguson/PhotoEdit

Cook, stirring constantly, until jelly melts. Remove from heat and stir in burgundy wine.

Poach pear halves in water, white wine, and sugar until cooked but still very firm, about 12 minutes.

Place the drained pears in a storage container. Pour the wine syrup over them, cover tightly and let stand overnight.

Pour pears into hot, sterilized jars and seal at once.

Spiced Orange Peel

*Utensils needed: Large glass bowl; Heavy
  kettle*
Preparation time: Allow 2 days
Quantity: About 3 4-ounce jars

4 cups sliced orange peel (from about 10 large clear-skinned oranges)	⅓ cup cider vinegar
	1 tablespoon whole cloves
	3 sticks cinnamon
1¾ cups sugar	

To prepare orange peel: Wash and dry oranges. Use a small paring knife to peel skin and a small amount of the white pith from the oranges in strips approximately 2½ x ½ inch. Measure peel and put into a large glass bowl. Cover with cold water and place in the refrigerator overnight.

Drain the cold water from the peel. Transfer peel to kettle, cover with fresh water and bring to a boil, uncovered, over high heat. As soon as peel boils, remove from heat and drain. Repeat. Then cover with water a third time and bring to a boil, simmer 10 minutes or until tender. Drain and set aside.

Put sugar, vinegar, cloves and cinnamon in same kettle and simmer 5 minutes to form a thick syrup. Add drained peel and simmer 5 minutes more, stirring frequently. Pour into hot, sterilized jars and seal at once.

Gala Spiced Fruit

Preheat oven to: 375 degrees
Utensils needed: Casserole dish
Baking time: 30 minutes

1 pound chopped dried apricots
½ pound chopped dried peaches
½ pound chopped dried pears
1 cup golden raisins
1 cup dark-brown sugar
1 teaspoon grated fresh lemon rind
¼ cup fresh lemon juice
¼ cup fresh orange juice
½ pound chopped dried figs

2 tablespoons brandy
2 cups dry white wine
½ teaspoon ground cinnamon
¼ teaspoon ground ginger
¼ teaspoon ground allspice
1 teaspoon minced crystallized ginger
1½ cups chopped pecans
½ cup unsalted butter

Mix all ingredients, except butter, together in a large mixing bowl. Cover and refrigerate at least 12 hours.

Remove from refrigerator. Stir to blend.

Butter a heavy casserole. Cut remaining butter into fruit and pour mixture into buttered casserole. Cover and bake at 375 degrees for about 30 minutes or until fruit is slightly caramelized.

Remove from oven and immediately pour into hot, sterilized jars and seal at once (see page 74).

Preserved Clementines

Preheat oven to: 350 degrees
Utensils needed: Covered casserole
Baking time: 1 hour
Quantity: 4 ½-pint jars

20 tiny Clementines free of blemishes	*¾ cup light corn syrup*
	1 cup sugar
water	*¼ cup brandy*

Simmer Clementines in water to cover for 20 minutes or until just soft. Cool in cooking water.

Pour off cooking water, measure and add more water if necessary to make 2 cups. Mix with corn syrup and sugar. Boil for 5 minutes. Add brandy.

Put Clementines into casserole and pour syrup over top. Cover and bake in preheated oven for 1 hour.

Pack into hot, sterilized jars and pour syrup over top. Seal at once.

© Michael Grand

3 pounds sugar	*1 teaspoon ground allspice*
1½ cups apple-cider vinegar	*1 teaspoon grated fresh ginger*
5 sticks cinnamon, broken	

Dip peaches in scalding-hot water for a few seconds. Slip off skins while hot. Stick 4 cloves in each peeled peach and place in large roaster.

Mix sugar, vinegar, cinnamon sticks and allspice in a bowl. Blend well and pour over the peaches. Cover with lid.

Place roaster in preheated oven. Cook peaches for 2 ½ hours without disturbing. Turn off heat; let peaches cool in roaster in oven.

When cool, pack cold in hot, sterilized jars. Fill with syrup to about ½ inch from top. Seal at once.

Spiced Peaches

Preheat oven to: 300 degrees
Utensils needed: Heavy roasting pan with lid
Baking time: 2½ hours
Quantity: About 8 1-quart jars

9 pounds medium-sized firm peaches	*4 whole cloves per peach*

Chutneys

Cranberry Chutney

Utensils needed: Heavy saucepan
Cooking time: 20 minutes
Quantity: About 8 4-ounce jars

1 cup yellow raisins
½ cup chopped dried
  pears
¼ cup chopped whole
  orange (including
  peel)
1 teaspoon grated
  fresh lemon rind
½ cup packed dark-
  brown sugar
½ cup fresh orange
  juice
¼ cup fresh lemon
  juice
½ cup water

3 cups washed and
  stemmed cranberries
1 cup cored and
  chopped tart green
  apple
1 teaspoon grated
  fresh ginger root
½ teaspoon minced
  Serrano chili
¼ cup chopped
  crystallized ginger
½ teaspoon ground
  cinnamon
¼ dried hot pepper
  flakes

Combine raisins, pears, orange, lemon rind, sugar, orange and lemon juices and water in heavy saucepan over medium heat. Bring to a boil, stirring constantly. Lower heat and simmer for 5 minutes.

Stir in cranberries, apple, fresh ginger and chili and simmer for another 10 minutes, stirring frequently. Stir in crystallized ginger, cinnamon and pepper flakes and cook for 5 minutes.

Pour into hot, sterilized jars and seal at once (see page 74).

Apple Chutney

Utensils needed: Food processor; Heavy
  saucepan
Cooking time: About 25 minutes
Quantity: About 10 4-ounce jars

5 cups apple slices
2 cups light-brown
  sugar
½ cup cider vinegar
1 cup slivered
  crystallized ginger
1 cup thinly sliced
  onion

2 cups white raisins
2 teaspoons chili
  powder
salt to taste
4 teaspoons mustard
  seeds
1 cup chopped
  walnuts

Chop the apples in the food processor using the metal blade and combine with the sugar, vinegar, ginger, onion, raisins, chili powder, salt and mustard seed. Bring to a boil and simmer about 30 minutes. Add walnuts. Pour into sterilized jars and seal at once (see page 74).

Onion Chutney

Utensils needed: Glass bowl
No cooking
Quantity: About 4 4-ounce jars
Storing: Refrigerator, tightly covered, up to 3 weeks

2 large Vidalia
onions
cold water

2 teaspoons cumin
seeds
salt to taste

© Brian Leatart

4 teaspoons chili
powder
dash Tabasco sauce
juice of 3 large
lemons

½ teaspoon grated
lemon rind
½ seeded and
minched jalapeño
pepper

Peel onions. Slice extremely thin and put into glass bowl. Fill bowl with cold water, stir onions (or rub with fingers) to wash well, then drain. Do this at least 5 times, draining after each washing.

Put drained onions back into bowl and rub cumin seed through palms of hands onto them. Add salt, chili powder and Tabasco. Mix well with wooden spoon. Pour on lemon juice. Add grated rind and jalapeño and mix again. Pour into hot, sterilized jars. Seal with paraffin. (Do not let chutney come into contact with metal.)

NOTE: Onion Chutney is exceptionally good with cold meats.

Pear Chutney

Utensils needed: Food processor; Heavy saucepan
Cooking time: 30 minutes
Quantity: 6 4-ounce jars

2½ pounds firm ripe
pears, washed and
cored
1 lemon, thinly sliced
½ cup raisins
¼ cup minced
crystallized ginger
½ cup cider vinegar

½ cup tightly packed
  brown sugar
¼ teaspoon ground
  nutmeg
½ teaspoon mustard
  seeds

1 teaspoon
  cornstarch
1 tablespoon water

Chop pears in the food processor using the metal blade.

Combine pears, lemon, raisins, ginger, brown sugar, vinegar, nutmeg, and mustard seed in saucepan, bring to a boil and simmer 25 minutes.

Blend cornstarch with 1 tablespoon water, add to mixture and cook over low heat, stirring until clear. Add diced pears and simmer 5 minutes more. Pour into hot, sterilized jars and seal at once.

Health Relish

Relishes and Pickles

© F. Stein/FPG International

We have chosen a sampling of the many different kinds of relishes and pickles that you can make. We have included fruit and vegetable relishes and pickles, using ingredients that are usually available throughout the year.

For large quantities of relishes and pickles, as well as for other recipes in this book, we suggest that you buy the produce from a farm stand out in the country rather than a local store. For the best results, you should use the very freshest vegetables that you can find. This is particularly true for cucumbers—if they are not fresh from the vine, they will not produce crisp pickles. Of course, the ulti-

mate satisfaction comes from pickling your own, home-grown vegetables.

Most of the recipes call for standard pint or half-pint jars. We prefer jars with screw-on lids—either those saved from other foods or those specially made for preserving. Again, if you are purchasing them, we recommend the canning jar with the two-part lid. They are easy to use and provide a tight seal.

For the best results in making the following recipes, you will need the same basic equipment that has been discussed on page 73. We also suggest that you have a pickling crock on hand, as some of the recipes call for one.

Relishes

5 green peppers
4 red peppers
2 large carrots
½ cup sugar (or to taste)
1 teaspoon celery seeds
coarse salt to taste
¼ teaspoon cayenne pepper

Wash all vegetables; then peel, trim or seed them. Coarsely chop in food processor using the metal blade. Squeeze out all juice and discard it.

Add remaining ingredients to the chopped vegetables and stir together until the sugar begins to dissolve.

Immediately pack into hot, sterilized jars and seal at once (see page 74)

© Brian Leatart

Health Relish

Utensils needed: Food processor; Large mixing bowl
No cooking
Quantity: About 10 8-ounce jars
Storing: Airtight containers, refrigerated, up to 2 weeks. Processed in boiling water bath for 15 minutes, up to 6 months.

1 large head cabbage
4 medium-sized onions
1 teaspoon mustard seeds
2 cups cider vinegar

Thai Cucumber Relish

Utensils needed: Medium and small saucepans
Cooking time: Approximately 2 minutes
Storing: Airtight containers, refrigerated, up to 2 weeks

2 cups diced carrots
1¼ cups white vinegar
⅓ cup sugar
1 tablespoon minced and seeded fresh jalapeño pepper
½ cup sliced scallion

1 large hothouse
cucumber, halved
lengthwise and
sliced very thin
crosswise

¼ cup grated fresh
coconut
¼ cup fresh lime juice
salt to taste

Blanch the carrots in a medium saucepan over medium heat until crisp and tender. Remove from heat. Drain and rinse in cold running water. Drain dry on paper towel.

In a small saucepan, bring vinegar and sugar to a boil over high heat. Boil, stirring constantly, until sugar is dissolved. Remove from heat and set aside.

Mix carrots, cucumber, scallion, coconut and lime juice together. Add vinegar, sugar and jalapeño pepper and stir to blend. Salt if desired.

Pour at once into hot, sterilized containers.

Spicy Cranberry Relish

Utensils needed: Food processor; Large bowl
No cooking
Quantity: About 4 cups
Storing: Airtight containers, refrigerated, up to 2 weeks. May be frozen

1 pound raw
cranberries
1 large tart apple
1 large, firm winter
pear
1 large juice orange
1 large lemon
1 cup sugar
½ small seeded
jalapeño pepper

1 grated fresh
gingerroot
1 teaspoon ground
cinnamon
½ teaspoon ground
cloves
1 teaspoon mustard
seeds
½ cup chopped
walnuts (optional)

Wash all fruit well. Quarter and seed all except cranberries. Chop all fruit together in the food processor using the metal blade. Pour into a large bowl. Do not lose juice.

Stir remaining ingredients into the chopped fruit. Mix well.

Place in covered jars or fancy containers. Store in refrigerator at least 24 hours before using.

Sun-Dried Tomato Relish

No cooking
Quantity: 8 4-ounce containers
Storing: Airtight containers, refrigerated, 2 weeks

1 cup chopped sun-
dried tomatoes
packed in oil
½ cup seeded and
minced green
pepper
2 cups whole kernel
corn (raw or
cooked)
¼ cup chopped
tomatillos
½ cup chopped red
onion

½ teaspoon seeded
and minced fresh
jalapeño pepper
2 tablespoons minced
fresh coriander
1 tablespoon minced
fresh parsley
2 tablespoons fresh
lime juice
1 tablespoon virgin
olive oil
salt to taste
pepper to taste

Mix all ingredients together. Stir to blend well. Add salt and pepper, if desired.

Pack into sterilized containers and seal at once.

Corn Relish

Utensils needed: Large heavy kettle
Cooking time: About 40 minutes
Quantity: About 16 8-ounce jars

2 quarts cut corn (about 18 to 20 ears)	1½ cups sugar
1 quart chopped cabbage	2 tablespoons ground mustard
1 cup seeded and chopped green pepper	1 tablespoon mustard seeds
1 cup seeded and chopped red pepper	1¼ tablespoons salt (optional or to taste)
2 large onions, chopped	¼ teaspoon cayenne pepper
1 quart cider vinegar	1 teaspoon ground turmeric
	1 cup water

Courtesy Dudley-Anderson-Yutzy

If corn is on cobs, boil for 5 minutes, dip in very cold water and cut from cob. Measure kernels.

Place all chopped vegetables and the corn in kettle and stir in all remaining ingredients. Place over medium heat, uncovered, and bring to a boil, stirring occasionally. Lower heat and simmer for 20 minutes.

Easy Relish

Utensils needed: Food processor
No cooking
Quantity: About 4 cups
Storing: Airtight container, refrigerated, up to 10 days

6 large red apples
2 medium red onions
2 stalks celery
4 large dill pickles
½ cup cider vinegar
½ cup sugar (or to taste)
½ teaspoon dry mustard

© Brian Leatart

Wash, core and quarter the apples. Peel the onions and cut in half. Wash the celery.

Combine all of these ingredients with the pickles and chop in food processor using the metal blade. Do not lose juice.

Add the vinegar, sugar and mustard to the ground mixture. Mix well.

Cover container and store in the refrigerator.

Pickles

Pickled Beets

Utensils needed: Heavy kettle
Cooking time: About 30 minutes
Quantity: About 4 8-ounce jars

8 cups tiny baby beets	*3 cups beet liquid*
or 5 bunches	*1 cup sugar*
washed raw beets	*2 cups cider vinegar*
or enough to make	*1 dozen whole cloves*
8 cups sliced cooked	*18 whole allspice*
beets	*½ teaspoon anise*
2 medium-size	*seeds*
Vidalia or Maui	*1½ teaspoons pickling*
onions or 2 cups	*spice per jar*
pearl onions	

Cook whole beets until just tender, about 1 hour. Drain, reserving 3 cups of the cooking liquid. Peel and slice the beets and set aside.

Peel the onions. Slice thin and separate into rings. Set aside.

Place the beet liquid, sugar, vinegar, anise seed, cloves and allspice in kettle over medium heat. Bring to a boil and add the sliced beets and onions. Again bring to a boil and boil for 5 minutes.

Place 1½ teaspoons pickling spice in the bottom of each hot, sterilized jar. Fill with beets and seal immediately.

Pickled Peaches

Utensils needed: Large covered bowl; Heavy
  kettle
Cooking time: About 25 minutes
Quantity: About 6 quart jars

7 pounds firm ripe	*¼ cup whole cloves,*
peaches	*heads removed,*
3 pounds sugar	*tied in cheesecloth*
1 quart cider vinegar	*bag*

Dip peaches in scalding-hot water for a few seconds, then immediately slip off skins. Place peaches in bowl, cover and set aside.

Place bag of cloves in kettle with the sugar and vinegar. Bring to a boil over medium heat and boil for about 15 minutes, or until clear and syrupy.

Put enough peaches to fill one jar into the boiling syrup. Cook until just beginning to get tender, about 5 minutes; do not overcook.

Lift peaches out of syrup with a slotted spoon, put into sterilized jar and put on lid to keep peaches hot. Continue this process until all jars are full. Pour boiling-hot syrup over peaches to about ½ inch from top of each jar and seal immediately.

NOTE: Any extra syrup may be kept for use as a glaze for ham or poultry.

© FPG International

Pickled Cauliflower

Utensils needed: Large glass container with
* cover; Large heavy kettle; Cheesecloth bag*
Preparation time: 2 days
Quantity: About 8 8-ounce jars

4 large fresh
  cauliflowers
	8 cups white-wine
	  vinegar

1 large red pepper (optional)	1 teaspoon mustard seeds
½ cup coarse salt	½ teaspoon celery seeds
2 cups sugar	6 whole white peppercorns

⅛ cup mixed pickling
  spice

1 tablespoon dried
  onion flakes

Wash cauliflower and break into florets. Dry well.
Place in glass container. If you are using red pepper, wash and seed it, cut into thin strips and add
to cauliflower. Sprinkle with 1 cup coarse salt.
Cover and let stand for 24 hours in a cool place.

Place salted cauliflower under cold running water. Wash thoroughly. Dry.

Place sugar, vinegar and spices (tied in a cheesecloth bag) in kettle. Bring to a boil over medium
heat. Boil gently, uncovered, for about 30 minutes.
Add cauliflower (and pepper, if used). Bring to boil
and boil for 5 minutes.

Pack into sterilized jars and seal.

Tuscan Onions

Utensils needed: Heavy saucepan
Cooking time: 12 minutes
Quantity: Approximately 8 8-ounce containers
Storing: Airtight containers, refrigerated, up to 8 weeks

¼ cup unsalted butter
¼ cup light-brown sugar
1 tablespoon grated fresh orange rind
3 pounds peeled pearl onions
2 cups fine white-wine vinegar
¼ cup balsamic vinegar
1 tablespoon fresh orange juice
2 cups water
¾ cup currants
2 cloves fresh garlic per container
3 whole cloves per jar
1 cinnamon stick per jar
approximately 2 cups virgin olive oil

Melt the butter.

In a heavy saucepan over medium heat, stir in the sugar. Cook, stirring constantly, until sugar dissolves and begins to caramelize. Add orange rind and onions. Stir to coat.

Pour in vinegars, orange juice and water and bring to a boil. Lower heat, stir in currants and simmer for 12 minutes or until onions are just tender but still holding their shape. Remove from heat and divide equal portions into sterilized containers. Add 2 cloves of fresh garlic, 3 whole cloves and 1 cinnamon stick to each container. Fill to top with olive oil. Seal at once. Do not use for at least 36 hours.

Cured Wild Mushrooms

Utensils needed: Heavy saucepan with lid; Small saucepan; Small crock with lid or sterilized jars
Cooking time: About 20 minutes
Quantity: About 6 8-ounce jars
Storing: Refrigerated, tightly covered, up to 3 months; sealed jars up to 1 year

3 pounds firm wild mushrooms
1 cup red-wine vinegar
coarse salt to taste
6 cloves garlic, mashed
4 bay leaves
¼ cup olive oil
2 teaspoons grated onion
1 tablespoon white peppercorns

Wipe mushrooms clean. If large, cut in half; if small, leave whole. Place in saucepan with ½ cup vinegar and salt. Cover and simmer gently for exactly 12 minutes.

In a small saucepan, combine 3 mashed garlic cloves, bay leaves, onion and remaining ½ cup vinegar. Bring to a boil over medium heat and boil for 3 minutes. Add to the simmered mushrooms and cook for about 3 minutes or until just tender.

Drain mushroom mixture well. Place in crock or sterilized jars. Add remaining 3 mashed garlic cloves, peppercorns and olive oil. Cover and place in the refrigerator.

Allow mushrooms to age 2 days. Then pack in sterilized jars and seal at once.

Pickled Haricot Vert

Utensils needed: *Saucepan*
Cooking time: *About 20 minutes*
Quantity: *3 4-ounce jars*

2 pounds very fresh haricot vert or tiny green beans	2 teaspoons fresh minced dill
1 cup vinegar	2 teaspoons mustard seeds
¼ cup water	1 teaspoon celery seeds
¼ cup sugar	
½ teaspoon Tabasco sauce	salt to taste

Wash and snap off ends of green beans. Simmer covered in boiling salted water until tender but still crisp.

Drain, cool and cut into ½-inch lengths. Cool thoroughly.

Mix vinegar, water, sugar, Tabasco sauce, dill, mustard seed, celery seed and salt in saucepan. Bring to boil and simmer, uncovered, 5 minutes. Add beans and bring to boil.

Spoon immediately into hot, sterilized jars and seal at once.

Green-Tomato Pickles

Utensils needed: *Sterilized canning jar with lid; Saucepan*
Cooking time: *Pickling solution: about 10 minutes*

Quantity: *1 quart*
Storing: *Room temperature, covered but unsealed, 1 week; sealed, indefinitely*

Approximately 10 to 12 1½-to-2-inch green tomatoes	2 small sweet red peppers
2 bay leaves	PICKLING SOLUTION:
1 teaspoon mixed pickling spice	4 cups water
1 large clove of garlic	2 cups mild vinegar
1 fresh dill stalk	½ cup salt

Wash tomatoes, remove stems and drain. Pack tightly into jar. Fill empty spaces with some quartered tomatoes. Add spices and peppers to jar. Place a stalk of fresh dill on top.

Bring pickling solution to boil. Pour while hot into filled jar. Seal at once.

Pickled Baby Carrots

Utensils needed: *Saucepan*
Preparation time: *About 1 hour*
Quantity: *About 4 8-ounce jars*

2 pounds baby carrots	1 teaspoon mustard seeds
2 cups water	1 tablespoon mixed pickling spice
2 cups Guinness stout or ale	¼ teaspoon cracked black pepper
2 cups cider vinegar	½ teaspoon coarse salt
½ cup sugar (or to taste)	

Wash and peel carrots. Place water and stout in saucepan and add carrots. Simmer, covered, for about 8 minutes, or until almost tender. Drain, reserving 2 cups of cooking liquid.

Put vinegar, cooking liquid, sugar and spices in saucepan. Bring to a boil over high heat and boil gently until mixture begins to get syrupy, about 15 minutes. Add cooked carrots to the syrup. Simmer gently, uncovered, for about 20 minutes.

Immediately pack into hot, sterilized jars and seal. Let stand about 2 weeks before use.

Vodka Pickles

Utensils needed: 2 heavy saucepans; Strainer
Cooking time: 5 minutes
Quantity: 6 8-ounce containers
Storing: Airtight containers, refrigerated, 6
*   months*

4 cups water	*2 cups baby plum*
1 cup diagonally	* tomatoes*
* sliced fresh carrot*	* (preferably yellow)*
* pieces*	*½ cup sugar*
½ cup green bell	*1¾ cups vodka*
* pepper pieces*	*¾ cup distilled water*
½ cup red bell pepper	*1 tablespoon whole*
* pieces*	* white peppercorns*
½ cup pearl onions	*½ teaspoon coarse*
½ cup peeled	* salt*
* sunchoke pieces*	

Bring 4 cups water to boil in heavy saucepan over high heat. Place all vegetables, except tomatoes, in a strainer and hold in boiling water for 1 minute. Mix these ingredients with the tomatoes and pack into sterilized containers. Cover and set aside.

Place sugar, vodka, water, peppercorns and salt in heavy saucepan over medium heat. Cook, stirring constantly, for about 5 minutes or until sugar is completely dissolved. Pour over vegetables to cover and seal at once.

© Ralph B. Pleasant/FPG International

Pickled Cherries

Utensils needed: Sterilized canning jar with
*   lid*
No cooking
Quantity: 1 quart

1 quart firm ripe	*½ teaspoon*
* cherries, stems on*	* coriander seeds*
1 tablespoon sugar	*½ cup balsamic*
1 teaspoon	* vinegar*
* peppercorns*	*water*
2 teaspoons salt	

Wash cherries well. Pack into sterilized quart jar. Add sugar, peppercorns, coriander, salt and vinegar. Fill jar to top with water. Seal at once.

Store at least 2 weeks before use.

NOTE: Use Pickled Cherries as you would olives or as a meat garnish or relish.

Marinated Olives, Flavored Vinegars, Salsa, Grainy Mustard, and Porcini Rice

Savories and Snacks

© Michael Grand

The term "Savories and Snacks" covers a variety of homemade gifts. It is a catchall of good things to add flavor and spice to ordinary ingredients—dips, spices, salad dressings and cocktail tidbits. Included here are flavored rices and nuts as well as cheeses and vinegars. People whose entertaining is most commonly a cocktail party are particularly receptive to these gifts. Bring several along to the next cocktail party you attend. Your hosts, and their guests, will be very grateful.

Here is where your imagination with packaging can really run wild. Rices can be put into small, colorful drawstring bags. An assortment of cocktail snacks can be packaged together on a serving tray. Cheeses can be packed in small crocks or shaped into balls or rolled into logs. Dips can be given with cheeses and crackers or homemade bread. We like to combine several gifts and use them for a housewarming present. They are always happily received and can be immediately enjoyed.

For decoration of jars, see the introduction to Jellies. You can use cottage-cheese containers wrapped in foil or decorated with colored tape. You can also purchase inexpensive containers at the dime store. Almost any packaging suggestion in this book can be applied to Savories and Snacks. Be creative with your packaging.

Nuts

Garlic Nuts

Preheat oven to: 325 degrees
Utensils needed: Shallow baking pan
Baking time: 20 to 25 minutes
Quantity: 4 cups
Storing: Airtight containers, in cool place, up to 6 weeks

| ¼ cup unsalted butter | ¼ teaspoon garlic powder |
| garlic salt to taste | 4 cups unblanched mixed nuts |

Melt butter in baking pan in oven. Blend in seasonings. Add almonds and bake 20 to 25 minutes, stirring frequently. Drain on paper towels. Cool before storing.

French-Fried Almonds

Utensils needed: Heavy iron frying pan
Frying time: 4 to 5 minutes
Quantity: 1 pound
Storing: Airtight container, in cool place, up to 6 weeks

| ¼ pound unsalted butter | 1 pound unblanched almonds |
| 2 tablespoons olive oil | seasoned salt to taste |

Melt the butter and olive oil in frying pan over medium-high heat. When melted, turn heat to low and pour in the almonds. Cook, stirring frequently, about 4 minutes or until almonds begin to brown.

With a slotted spoon, remove almonds from butter. Drain on paper towel or a paper bag. When well drained, sprinkle with seasoned salt to taste. Cool before storing.

Curried Almonds

Preheat oven to: 300 degrees
Utensils needed: Shallow baking pan
Baking time: 45 minutes
Quantity: 2 cups
Storing: Airtight container, in cool place, up to 6 weeks

2 cups whole almonds, blanched	1 tablespoon curry powder
¼ cup unsalted butter	dash ground cumin
seasoned salt to taste	1 teaspoon grated fresh orange rind

Spread nuts in shallow baking pan. Bake at 300 degrees for 25 minutes or until golden.

Melt butter in skillet and stir in seasoned salt, curry powder, cumin and orange rind. Pour over nuts and continue roasting, stirring occasionally, about 20 minutes. Remove from oven and spread on paper towels to drain. Cool before storing.

Chili Nuts

Preheat oven to: 300 degrees
Utensils needed: Roasting pan
Baking time: 45 minutes
Quantity: 4 cups
Storing: Airtight container, in cool place, up
*   to 6 weeks*

2 cups cashews
2 cups pecans
¼ cup unsalted
    butter
2 teaspoons chili
    powder

¼ teaspoon cayenne
    pepper (or to taste)
½ teaspoon garlic
    salt (or to taste)
dash Tabasco sauce

Spread nuts in roasting pan. Toast in preheated oven for 25 minutes, stirring occasionally.

Melt butter in skillet and add chili powder, cayenne, garlic salt and Tabasco. Pour over nuts and roast, stirring frequently, for 20 minutes. Drain on paper towels. Cool before storing.

Whole Roasted Walnuts

Preheat oven to: 350 degrees
Utensils needed: Shallow baking pan
Baking time: 25 minutes
Quantity: As many pounds as you wish to
*   prepare*
Storing: Airtight container, in cool place, up
*   to 6 months*

walnuts

Place unshelled walnuts in baking pan and bake at 350 degrees for exactly 25 minutes. Cool before storing.

NOTE: This is the simplest recipe we know. When roasted, walnuts have a superb toasty taste.

Appetizers

Bean Dip

Utensils needed: Stock pot; Heavy earthenware bean pot
Preparation time: Allow 2 days
Quantity: About 2 quarts
Storing: Tightly covered container, refrigerated, 1 week. May be frozen

4 cups pinto beans	½ pound sharp
water to cover	cheddar cheese,
2 cups chopped	grated
onions	Tabasco sauce to
3 cloves garlic,	taste
mashed	salt to taste
½ small seeded and	
minced jalapeño	
pepper	
2 teaspoons ground	
cumin seed	
6 tablespoons bacon	
fat	
5 tablespoons chili	
powder	
1 cup unsalted butter	

Wash beans thoroughly. Place in stock pot and cover with water. Let soak overnight.

Add onions, garlic, jalapeño, cumin and bacon fat to soak beans. Place over medium heat and bring to a boil. Lower heat and simmer, stirring frequently, three to four hours, until beans are very, very soft. If additional liquid is needed, add ½ cup boiling water at a time.

When beans are soft, add the chili powder and cook for about 5 minutes, stirring constantly. Using a potato masher or large wooden spoon, mash in the butter, cheese, Tabasco and salt. Blend until smooth.

Cover tightly, let cool, and store in cooking pot in refrigerator or in plastic freezer containers in the freezer.

NOTE: This dip is to be served warm with corn chips, tortillas or bread sticks. May also be used as a filling for burritos, tacos, enchiladas or tostadas.

Brandied Blue Cheese

Utensils needed: Mixing bowl; Wire whisk
No cooking
Quantity: About 1 pound
Storing: Airtight container, refrigerated, up to 1 month

¾ pound soft Maytag	2 tablespoons brandy
blue cheese	¼ cup chopped
¼ cup soft unsalted	toasted almonds
butter	

Combine blue cheese, butter and brandy in mixing bowl and beat with wire whisk until smooth. Stir in almonds. Pack into a cheese crock or 4-ounce jars, seal with paraffin (see page 74) and refrigerate.

Caponata

Utensils needed: Heavy frying pan
Cooking time: About 25 minutes
Quantity: About 4 pounds
Storing: Tightly covered container, refrigerated, up to 6 weeks

2 pounds eggplant, cubed
½ cup olive oil
4 large tomatoes, peeled and chopped
3 large green peppers, chopped
3 large onions, chopped
2 cups pitted green olives
½ cup wine vinegar
1 tablespoon sugar (optional)
½ teaspoon minced fresh oregano
½ teaspoon minced fresh basil
¼ cup water

Sauté eggplant cubes in olive oil over medium-high heat for about 15 minutes, stirring frequently. Add tomatoes, peppers, onions and olives. Cook for about 10 minutes. Remove from heat.

Mix together the vinegar, sugar, oregano, basil and water. Stir to dissolve the sugar. Add to vegetable mixture.

Pour into covered storage container. Chill in the refrigerator at least 12 hours before using.

This is an excellent appetizer or can be used as a cold vegetable dish.

© Charles Schneider/FPG International

Hoummus

Utensils needed: Food processor
No cooking
Quantity: About 3 cups
Storing: Refrigerated, tightly covered, up to 1 week

3 1-pound cans chickpeas
8 cloves garlic
juice of 6 lemons
salt to taste
1 1-pound can tahini (ground sesame seed—available in imported food shops)

Drain chick-peas, reserving liquid. Blend the drained chick-peas, tahina and garlic in the food processor using the metal blade. Add up to 1 cup reserved chick-pea liquid and juice of 6 lemons. Salt to taste and mix well.

Pack into decorative jars or crocks and store in the refrigerator.

NOTE: Hoummus may be given with Cuban Bread (page 26) or the traditional pita bread.

Salsa

Utensils needed: Food processor
No cooking
Quantity: About 4 8-ounce containers
Storing: Airtight containers, refrigerated, up to 1 week

8 husked and quartered medium tomatillos	½ seeded and sliced green pepper
3 cored and quartered medium tomatoes	½ cup fresh coriander leaves
1 peeled and quartered medium onion	1 seeded and sliced serrano (or jalapeño) chili
3 peeled and halved cloves garlic	juice of 1 lime
4 trimmed scallions (greens included)	salt (optional or to taste)
	pepper to taste

Chop all ingredients in food processor using the metal blade, making on-and-off turns until you obtain a chunky mixture.

Pour into sterilized containers. Cover and refrigerate at least 6 hours before using.
VARIATION:
For salt-free diets, add about ½ teaspoon sugar to bring out sauce's flavor. For sugar-free diets, add 1 teaspoon frozen apple-juice concentrate.

NOTE: This sauce can be used as a dip for tortilla chips or as a condiment for Southwestern foods.

Meat or Poultry Pastries

For pastry recipe: See Jam Pastries in Chaper 3 (page 48).

MEAT OR POULTRY FILLING

Utensils needed: Heavy frying pan
Cooking time: About 15 minutes
Quantity: About 5 dozen

⅛ pound butter	½ teaspoon minced fresh thyme (for meat) or minced fresh tarragon (for poultry)
2 cups ground, cooked meat or poultry	
⅛ cup grated onion	
⅛ cup grated celery	salt to taste
1 tablespoon fresh chopped parsley	cracked black pepper to taste

Melt butter in frying pan over low heat. Add all other ingredients and cook until onion and celery are soft and translucent—about 15 minutes. Do not overcook, as filling will become too dry.

Fill and bake as for Jam Pastries. These may be frozen and warmed slightly when ready to serve.

Marinated Olives

No cooking
Quantity: 1 8-ounce jar
Storing: Airtight container, refrigerated, up
  to 2 months

1 8-ounce screw-top
  jar ripe or green
  olives with pits
olive oil
red-wine vinegar

1 clove garlic,
  crushed
¼ teaspoon cracked
  black pepper
1 bay leaf

Drain all juice from olives and discard, leaving olives in jar. Fill jar two-thirds full with olive oil. Fill to the top with wine vinegar. Add the crushed garlic, pepper and bay leaf. Screw on lid and shake vigorously to mix. Allow to blend in the refrigerator at least 2 days before use.

Marinated Chèvre

No cooking time
Quantity: 6 wide-mouth 4-ounce containers
Storing: Airtight containers, refrigerated, up
  to 1 month

6 4-ounce goat-cheese
  buttons or 12
  2-ounce goat-cheese
  buttons
3 cups virgin olive oil

12 peeled cloves garlic
6 sprigs fresh oregano
6 sprigs fresh thyme
6 sprigs fresh tarragon
6 strips orange peel

Place goat-cheese buttons in sterilized wide-mouth containers. Do not crush. Cover with olive oil. Add 2 cloves of garlic, 1 sprig each of oregano, thyme, tarragon and 1 strip of orange peel to each container. Cover at once. Do not use for at least 24 hours.

Anchoiade

Utensils needed: Food processor
No cooking time
Quantity: About 3 4-ounce containers
Storing: Airtight containers, refrigerated, up
  to 1 month

12 ounces anchovy
  fillets packed in
  olive oil
2 tablespoons mashed
  fresh garlic
1 tablespoon minced
  red onion

1 cup chopped fresh
  parsley
⅓ cup red-wine
  vinegar

Using the metal blade and making quick on-and-off turns, quickly blend all ingredients in the food processor to make a coarse mixture.
  Pack into sterilized containers and seal at once.

NOTE: This should be served warm on toasted baguette slices or crisp crackers.

Tangy Cheese Pot

Utensils needed: Electric blender or mixer; Small crocks or jars with tight lids
No cooking
Quantity: About 3 cups
Storing: Airtight containers, refrigerated, up to 1 month.

1 pound grated cheddar cheese
⅓ cup sherry wine

1 tablespoon peanut oil
1 teaspoon chopped fresh chives

1 teaspon Dijon mustard
dash cayenne pepper

onion salt to taste
1 teaspoon curry powder

For electric blender: Blend half of the cheese and all the remaining ingredients on medium speed until smooth. Add remaining cheese and blend until smooth. If too thick, add up to ¼ cup more sherry.

For electric mixer: Place all ingredients in mixing bowl.

Beat at medium speed until well-blended. If mixture is lumpy, use a large wooden spoon to smooth.

Place in storage containers and store as directed.

For Salads

Salad Seasoning

Utensils needed: Mixing bowl
No cooking
Quantity: About 3¼ cups
Storing: Airtight container, in cool place, up to 3 months

2 cups finely grated Parmesan cheese
2 teaspoons coarse salt (or to taste)
½ cup sesame seeds, lightly toasted

¼ cup poppy seeds
3 tablespoons celery seeds
½ teaspoon garlic salt
1 tablespoon dried onion flakes

2 tablespoons parsley flakes
½ teaspoon dried dill

1 teaspoon paprika
½ teaspoon cracked black pepper

Combine all ingredients in a mixing bowl and stir to blend well. Pour into storage container, cover tightly and store in a cool place.

NOTE: For gift giving, attach these directions: Sprinkle 1 to 2 tablespoonfuls on salad greens, as a seasoning with a plain oil-and-vinegar dressing.

Salad Seasoning is also good in cream sauces and as a garnish on baked potatoes.

Oil de Provence

Utensils needed: Mixing bowl
No cooking
Quantity: 1 quart
Storing: Airtight containers, refrigerated, up to 1 month

1 quart grape-seed oil (any high-quality oil will do)
1 teaspoon minced fresh marjoram
1 teaspoon minced fresh thyme
1 teaspoon minced fresh savory

10 tiny red-bird peppers (or any tiny hot red or green pepper)
1 teaspoon cracked black pepper

Mix all ingredients together. Cover and let set at least 24 hours before using.

© Brian Leatart

Three Vinegars

Quantity: 1 pint
Storing: Cool, dark place

TARRAGON VINEGAR

1 pint fine-wine vinegar
3 sprigs fresh tarragon

Combine vinegar and tarragon and let stand 3 weeks. Remove tarragon.

GARLIC VINEGAR

1 pint fine-wine vinegar
3 cloves garlic

Add garlic to vinegar and let stand 1 week. Remove garlic.

DILL VINEGAR

1 pint fine-wine vinegar
3 sprigs fresh dill

Combine vinegar and dill and let stand 3 weeks. Remove dill.

Fruit-Salad Dressing

Utensils needed: Electric blender or rotary beater
No cooking
Quantity: About 2 cups
Storing: Airtight container, refrigerated, up to 2 weeks

1 cup fresh orange juice
1 cup peanut oil
2 tablespoons honey
2 tablespoons fresh lemon juice

¼ teaspoon ground nutmeg
½ teaspoon salt

Combine all ingredients and blend for a few seconds at high speed in an electric blender, or beat with a rotary beater until well-combined.

Pour into storage container, cover tightly, and refrigerate.

Herbed Croutons

Preheat oven to: 400 degrees
Utensils needed: Shallow baking pan
Baking time: About 7 minutes
Quantity: About 4 cups
Storing: Airtight container, in cool place, up to 1 month

½ cup unsalted margarine

1 tablespoon olive oil
1 teaspoon onion salt

1 teaspoon minced fresh marjoram
½ teaspoon minced fresh chervil
¼ teaspoon minced fresh thyme

1 teaspoon minced fresh parsley
4 cups toasted dried bread cubes

Melt margarine and olive oil in baking pan in oven. Remove from oven and add spices and bread cubes; stir until well-coated with melted oil.

Return to oven and bake for about 5 minutes, watching to see that croutons do not burn. As soon as they take on a medium-brown color, remove from heat. Cool on paper towel.

Place in storage container, cover and store in a cool place. These may also be stored in plastic bags.

NOTE: Herbed Croutons are excellent in soups as well as salads.

Mollie's Special Salad Dressing

Utensils needed: Electric blender
No cooking
Quantity: About 2 cups
Storing: Airtight container, refrigerated, up to 2 weeks

1 6-ounce can tomato paste
6 ounces red-wine vinegar
6 ounces vegetable oil

1 medium-size onion, coarsely chopped
1 egg
salt to taste
pepper to taste

Empty can of tomato paste into blender jar. Fill empty can with vinegar and add to tomato paste. Refill can with vegetable oil and add to the tomato paste and vinegar. Add onion and egg. Blend at high speed for about 10 seconds. Add salt and pepper and whirl just to blend. Pour into storage container, cover tightly and refrigerate.

Seasonings

Curry Powder

Preheat oven to: 250 degrees
Utensils needed: Flat baking dish or cookie sheet; Electric blender
Baking time: 15 minutes
Quantity: About 1¼ pounds
Storing: Airtight container, in cool place, up to 6 months

1 pound coriander seeds
¼ pound small cumin seeds
1 tablespoon ginger root
1 dried hot pepper pod
1 tablespoon sweet cumin seeds

1 tablespoon mustard seeds
1 cinnamon stick, about 2 inches long
1 teaspoon whole cloves
2 cardamon seeds
8 black peppercorns

Place all ingredients on baking pan, spreading to cover bottom. Bake at 250 degrees for about 15 minutes or until the spices are very hot. Remove from heat and immediately pour into blender container. Blend, while spices are still hot, for a few seconds at high speed.

Pack into jars with tight lids and store in a cool place.

NOTE: You may wish to accompany a gift of home-made curry powder with recipes for different curry dishes.

Seasoned Salt

Utensils needed: Mixing bowl
Quantity: About 1½ cups
Storing: Airtight container, in cool place, up
to 6 months

1 cup coarse salt	1 teaspoon curry
1 teaspoon dried	powder
thyme	2 teaspoons dry
1½ teaspoons dried	mustard
oregano	½ teaspoon onion
1½ teaspoons garlic	powder
powder	¼ teaspoon dill weed
2 teaspoons paprika	

Combine all ingredients in mixing bowl and stir to blend well. Pour into storage container, cover tightly and store in a cool place.

Seasoned Pepper

Utensils needed: Mixing bowl
No cooking
Quantity: 4 4-ounce containers
Storing: Airtight containers, cool place
indefinitely

¾ cup cracked black	¼ cup dried onion
pepper	flakes
1 tablespoon cayenne	2 tablespoons garlic
pepper	powder

2 tablespoons dried	2 tablespoons coarse
lemon rind	salt (optional)
½ cup dark-brown	½ cup sweet paprika
sugar	

Combine all ingredients. Pack into sterilized containers and seal at once.

NOTE: This is used to flavor meats or poultry, for roasting, broiling or barbecuing.

Oriental Peanut Sauce

Utensils needed: Food processor
No cooking
Quantity: 7 4-ounce containers
Storing: Airtight containers, up to 2 weeks

2 cups smooth	chicken broth
peanut butter	1 teaspoon chili oil
1 tablespoon fresh	(or to taste)
coconut milk	
1 teaspoon fresh	
lemon juice	
¼ cup soy sauce	
4 cloves garlic	
1 teaspoon honey	
1 cup homemade	

© Horcastas/FPG International

Combine all ingredients. In a food processor, using the metal blade, process until well blended.

Pour into sterilized containers and seal at once.

NOTE: This may be used as the sauce on Oriental cold noodles or as a sauce for cold poultry or fresh fish.

1 teaspoon salt
1 cup beer
½ cup apple-cider
vinegar
1 cup water
¼ teaspoon ground
cloves

¼ teaspoon ground
allspice
dash Tabasco
⅛ cup orange-
blossom or other
fragrant honey

In a heavy saucepan, over high heat, bring all ingredients, except honey, to a boil. Remove from heat and pour into food processor. Using the metal blade, process until just blended, about 1 minute. Add honey and process to blend.

Pour into sterilized containers and cover at once. Wait at least 12 hours before using.

Sesame Marinade

Utensils needed: Mixing bowl

No cooking
Quantity: Approximately 6 4-ounce containers
Storing: Airtight containers, up to 1 month

1½ cups sesame seeds
1 cup soy sauce
½ cup vegetable oil
¼ cup honey
¼ cup fresh orange
juice

1 teaspoon Tabasco
sauce (or to taste)
1 teaspoon grated
fresh orange rind

Blend all ingredients together. Pour into sterilized containers and cover at once.

NOTE: This is a tasty marinade for poultry or pork.

Hot-and-Sweet Mustard

Utensils needed: Food processor; Heavy saucepan
Cooking time: Approximately 1 minute
Quantity: Approximately 3 8-ounce containers
Storing: Airtight containers, refrigerated, up to 3 months

¾ cup mustard seeds
½ cup tightly packed
light-brown sugar
2 teaspoons minced
fresh garlic

1 cup dry mustard
1 teaspoon minced
fresh tarragon
1 teaspoon minced
fresh horseradish

Pesto

Utensils needed: *Food processor*
No cooking
Quantity: *About 4 4-ounce containers*
Storing: *Airtight containers, refrigerated, up to 2 weeks*

2 teaspoons minced fresh garlic
1 tablespoon fresh lemon juice
1 cup freshly grated Parmesan cheese

1 cup shelled, unsalted roasted pistachios (or toasted pine nuts)
2 cups tightly packed fresh basil leaves

¼ cup loosely packed parsley leaves
1 cup extra-virgin olive oil

salt to taste

Place garlic, lemon juice, nuts, cheese, basil and parsley in food processor fitted with a metal blade. Making quick on-and-off turns, chop until mixture is finely ground. With machine running, pour in about ¾ cup of olive oil and mix until mixture is consistency of mayonnaise.

Pack into sterilized containers and cover with a thin layer of olive oil. Seal at once.

NOTE: This can be used on pasta, vegetable salads, fresh tomatoes or on toasted Italian peasant bread. It can also be used as a dip for crudités.

Flavored Rices

Porcini Rice

Utensils needed: *Mixing bowl*
No cooking
Quantity: *About 4 cups*
Storing: *Airtight containers, in cool place, up to 6 months*

1 tablespoon powdered beef bouillon

4 cups uncooked rice
1 cup chopped dried porcini

1 teaspoon dried thyme
2 teaspoons dried parsley

¼ teaspoon cracked black pepper

Mix all ingredients together in mixing bowl. Divide equally into four containers—jars with lids or plastic bags. Seal airtight.

NOTE: Along with this gift, be sure to attach cooking directions. The cooking time of flavored rices remains unchanged from that given on whatever kind of rice you use.

Onion Rice

Utensils needed: Mixing bowl
No cooking
Quantity: About 4 cups
Storing: Airtight containers, in cool place, up
to 6 months

- *4 cups uncooked rice*
- *¼ cup dried onion flakes*
- *½ teaspoon garlic powder*
- *¼ teaspoon celery seeds*
- *½ teaspoon coarse salt*
- *1 teaspoon dried parsley*

Mix all ingredients together in mixing bowl. Divide equally into four containers—jars with lids or plastic bags. Seal airtight.

Chicken or Lemon Rice

Utensils needed: Mixing bowl
No cooking
Quantity: About 4 cups
Storing: Airtight containers, in cool place, up
to 6 months

- *4 cups uncooked rice*
- *4 tablespoons powdered chicken bouillon*
- *2 teaspoons dried tarragon*
- *2 teaspoons dried chopped chives*
- *¼ teaspoon ground white pepper*

Mix all ingredients together in mixing bowl. Divide equally into four containers—jars with lids or plastic bags. Seal airtight.

VARIATION:

For Lemon Rice, substitute 1 ½ tablespoons grated lemon rind, 2 teaspoons dried parsley, and ½ teaspoon cracked black pepper for the last 3 ingredients of Chicken Rice.

Festive Beverages

© Brian Leatart

The beverages that we have included are very special ones. As gifts, they are superb given alone or may be accompanied by homemade extras: for instance, Spiced Tea with a Tea Bread; Mocha Coffee with any delicious cake; Coffee Liqueur with a tray of after-dinner tidbits.

The Spiced Teâ is most attractive packaged in a small tea canister. It can, of course, also be packaged in plastic bags or tightly-covered jars. Mocha Coffee is most easily packaged in the instant-coffee jar from which you have taken the coffee for the recipe. A bag of cinnamon sticks is a good addition to either of these.

Coffee Liqueur is best made and given in a clean (and odorless) half-gallon wine bottle. This type of bottle is usually so attractive that additional trim is not necessary, except perhaps a fancy bow.

Festive Beverages

¼ cup whole cloves
1 tablespoon chopped
crystallized ginger

1 teaspoon grated
nutmeg (or to
taste)

Combine all ingredients in mixing bowl and stir to blend well. Pour mixture into tea canisters or any other type of container with a tight lid.

Coffee Liqueur

Utensils needed: Heavy saucepan; Clean, odorless ½-gallon glass bottle with cap
Cooking time: About 10 minutes
Quantity: About ½ gallon
Storing: Airtight container, in cool place, up to 6 months

2 cups boiling water
3 cups granulated
sugar
1 2-ounce jar instant-
coffee powder

1 fifth vodka or
bourbon
1 large vanilla bean,
cut into small
pieces

Combine 1 cup boiling water and the sugar in saucepan. Cook uncovered over medium heat, without stirring, for about 10 minutes to make a thin syrup.

Spiced Tea

Utensils needed: Mixing bowl
No cooking
Quantity: About 2 cups
Storing: Airtight containers, in cool place, up to 6 months

½ pound orange
pekoe tea
2 tablespoons ground
dried orange peel

1 tablespoon ground
dried lemon peel
2 cinnamon sticks,
crushed

© Brian Leatart

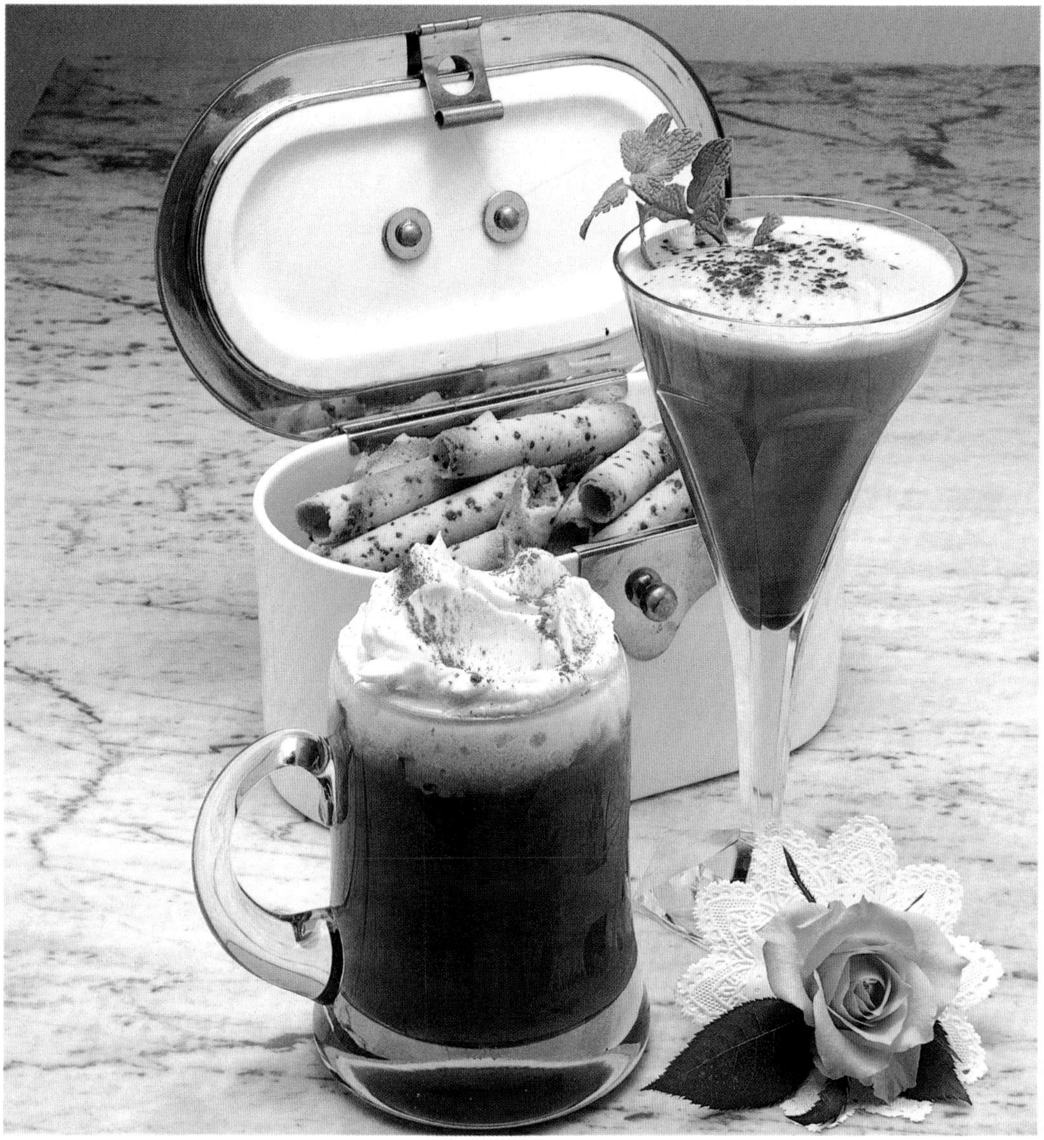

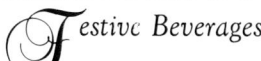

Add 1 cup boiling water to the instant-coffee powder and stir to dissolve. Add the coffee to the syrup.

Remove from heat and cool to lukewarm. Stir in the vodka or bourbon and the vanilla bean. Pour into the clean ½-gallon bottle. Cap tightly.

Store at least 3 weeks before using. The longer Coffee Liqueur stands, the better it is.

Flavored Vodka

Utensils needed: At least one 1-quart, nonmetallic container with tight-fitting lid; Fine sieve
No cooking
Quantity: 1 quart
Storing: Airtight container, in cool place, indefinitely

© Lohman/FPG International

Citrus Vodka

1 quart vodka
2 tablespoons grated fresh lemon rind
1 tablespoon grated fresh orange rind
1 whole lemon, sliced

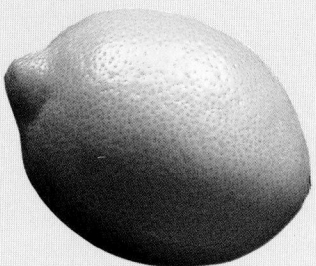

Place vodka in a nonmetallic container that has a tightly fitted lid. Add lemon and orange rind and sliced lemon to vodka. Cover and store in a cool place for 1 week. Strain the vodka through a fine sieve and pour into sterilized container. Seal at once.

NOTE: You may, if desired, place 2 fresh hot peppers or a sprig of dill or pieces of citrus rind into appropriate vodka for garnish.

Hot Chili Pepper Vodka

1 quart vodka
6 small dried hot chili peppers

Place vodka in a nonmetallic container that has a tightly fitted lid. Crush 2 hot peppers and add all peppers to vodka. Cover and store in a cool place for 1 week. Strain the vodka through a fine sieve and pour into sterilized container. Seal at once.

Black Pepper Vodka

1 quart vodka
2 tablespoons cracked
  black pepper
3 sprigs fresh dill

Place vodka in a nonmetallic container that has a tightly fitted lid. Add cracked black pepper and fresh dill to vodka. Cover and store in a cool place for 1 week. Strain the vodka through a fine sieve and pour into sterilized container. Seal at once.

Cranberry Cordial

Utensils needed: Food processor; Fine sieve;
  At least one 1-quart nonmetallic container
  with tight-fitting lid
No cooking
Quantity: 1 quart
Storing: Airtight container, in cool place,
  indefinitely

  2 cups superfine
    sugar
  2 cups vodka (or gin)
  6 whole cloves
  1 strip fresh orange
    peel
  4 cups fresh
    cranberries

Mix the sugar and liquor in a nonmetallic container that has a tightly fitting cover. Stir to blend. Add cloves and orange peel.

Finely chop cranberries in a food processor using the metal blade. Mix into the sugared liquor. Stir to blend.

Cover and store in a cool place, shaking or stirring once a day for 2 weeks.

Strain the mixture through a fine sieve, pressing to extract all liquid. Pour into sterilized quart jar and seal at once.

Part Five

Low-Calorie & Special Diet Foods

Low-Calorie Carrot Cake

A Bit of Everything

© Steven Mark Needham/Envision

This section can provide a variety of gifts for those on restricted diets or for those simply interested in extra healthy eating.

Here, we've included, well, "A Bit of Everything." There are recipes for chutney, cakes, syrup, dressing, muffins and more — all designed to be as healthy as they are delicious.

For packaging, refer back to the respective introductions for each individual category.

Mixed-Fruit Chutney

Utensils needed: Heavy saucepan
Cooking time: Approximately 10 minutes
Quantity: 8 8-ounce containers
Storing: Airtight containers, refrigerated, up to 4 weeks

⅓ cup raisin
⅓ cup currants
½ teaspoon red hot pepper flakes
¾ cup raspberry vinegar
2 tablespoons frozen apple-juice concentrate
1 cup chopped red onion
2 teaspoons minced garlic
1 teaspoon grated orange rind
1 teaspoon ground cinnamon
4 cups chopped green tomatoes
1 tablespoon fresh lemon juice
2 cups fresh blueberries
1 cup chopped very ripe apricots, nectarines or peaches
1 cup chopped very ripe mango
dash Tabasco sauce (or to taste)

In a heavy saucepan, bring the raisins, currants, pepper flakes, vinegar and apple juice to a boil over high heat. Lower heat and add onion, garlic, orange rind and cinnamon. Simmer for 5 minutes. Add green tomatoes and lemon juice and simmer for 5 more minutes.

Remove from heat and stir in remaining fruit and Tabasco, if desired.

Pour into sterilized containers and seal at once.

All-Fruit Jam

Utensils needed: Kettle
Cooking time: About 5 minutes
Quantity: 6 8-ounce jars

4 cups peeled, pitted and chopped very ripe fresh fruit
1 cup peeled, pitted and chopped barely ripe fresh fruit
⅓ cup frozen apple-juice concentrate
3 tablespoons white grape juice
2 teaspoons fresh lemon juice
1 teaspoon pure vanilla extract (optional)
3 tablespoons liquid pectin

Place all ingredients in a kettle over high heat. Bring to a boil, lower heat and simmer, stirring frequently, for 5 minutes.

Remove from heat. Pour into sterilized jars and seal at once. Let set for at least 24 hours before using.

Fresh-Fruit Syrup

*Utensils needed: Blender or food processor;
Heavy saucepan*
Cooking time: About 5 minutes
Quantity: 8 4-ounce containers
Storing: Airtight containers

6 cups crushed very ripe sweet fruit (any berries, apricots, peaches), pitted, if necessary	1 teaspoon pure vanilla extract
1 cup frozen apple-juice concentrate	1 teaspoon fresh lemon juice
1 tablespoon fresh orange juice	¼ teaspoon ground cinnamon
	dash ground nutmeg
	3 tablespoons cornstarch

Blend all ingredients together in blender or food processor until well-combined. (Strain through a fine colander if using berries and a seedless syrup is desired.)

Pour into a heavy saucepan and bring to a boil over high heat. Lower heat and simmer, stirring constantly, for 5 minutes or until slightly thickened.

Pour into hot, sterilized containers and seal at once.

Low-Calorie Salad Dressing

Utensils needed: Heavy saucepan; Blender
Quantity: 4 4-ounce containers
Storing: Airtight containers, refrigerated, up to 4 weeks

½ cup cold water	¼ cup minced red onion
1 cup white grape juice	1 teaspoon dry mustard powder
½ cup fruit-flavored vinegar (such as raspberry)	1½ teaspoons chopped fresh herbs of your choice (can be one or any combination of favorites)
1 teaspoon frozen apple-juice concentrate	
1 tablespoon fresh lemon juice	
1 teaspoon light soy sauce	dash cayenne pepper
2 teaspoons minced garlic	1 tablespoon liquid pectin
	1 teaspoon arrowroot

In a heavy saucepan bring all ingredients to a boil over high heat. Lower heat and simmer, stirring constantly, for about 5 minutes or until slightly thickened. Remove from heat and pour into a blender.

Blend until well-combined. Pour into sterilized containers and seal at once.

NOTE: Special thanks to the Pritikin Diet for inspiration.

© J. Trefether/FPG International

Marinated Peppers

Utensils needed: Mixing bowl
Quantity: 6 4-ounce containers
Storing: Airtight containers, refrigerated, up
  to 4 weeks

6 large green peppers
6 large red peppers
¼ cup fresh garlic
  slices
2 teaspoons minced
  red onion
salt to taste (optional)

¼ teaspoon crushed
  red pepper flakes
¼ cup extra-virgin
  olive oil (or any
  other high-quality
  vegetable oil)

Roast peppers over open gas flame or under the broiler flame until well blackened on all sides. Place in plastic bags and seal for about 10 minutes to steam off charred skin. Peel and seed, keeping as much of the juice as possible.

Cut peppers into chunks and place in mixing bowl. Stir in all other ingredients. Pack into sterilized containers and seal at once. Allow to set at least 24 hours before using.

Pickled Vegetables

Utensils needed: Heavy saucepan
Cooking time: Approximately 25 minutes
Quantity: 6 8-ounce containers
Storing: Airtight containers, refrigerated, up
  to 6 weeks

3 cups white-wine
  vinegar
1 cup rice-wine
  vinegar
1 cup apple-cider
  vinegar
2 cups water
½ cup frozen apple-
  juice concentrate
2 strips fresh lemon
  peel
1 tablespoon whole
  cloves
6 whole cloves garlic
¾ cup pickling spice
½ teaspoon fresh
  ground pepper
1 tablespoon chopped
  fresh dill

6 small Kirby (or
  pickling)
  cucumbers
2 cups very small
  cauliflower florets
2 cups seeded and
  cubed red bell
  peppers
2 cups seeded and
  cubed yellow bell
  peppers
1 cup peeled and
  sliced carrots
1 cup pearl onions
½ cup balsamic
  vinegar
6 fresh dill sprigs

Place vinegars, water, apple juice, lemon peel, cloves, garlic, pickling spice, pepper and chopped dill in large heavy saucepan over high heat. Bring to a boil and lower heat and simmer for 15 minutes. Add vegetables and cook for about 5 minutes or until tender but still crisp.

Pack vegetables into sterilized containers. Return liquid to heat. Add balsamic vinegar and boil for 5 minutes.

Immediately pour over vegetables. Add 1 dill sprig to each container and seal at once.

Unprocessed Bran Muffins

Preheat oven to: 350 degrees
Utensils needed: Blender; Medium-sized bowl; 1 12-cup muffin pan coated with nonstick spray
Baking time: 30 minutes

½ cup water	1 teaspoon pure
½ cup powdered skim	vanilla extract
milk	1 teaspoon baking
3 large eggs	powder
1½ cups grated fresh	1 teaspoon baking
zucchini	soda
1 teaspoon ground	8–9 packets of
cinnamon	aspartame
1 teaspoon pumpkin-	sweetener
pie spice	2 cups unprocessed
1 teaspoon ground	bran, either coarse
nutmeg	or fine grind
¼ teaspoon ground	
ginger	

In blender, combine water, milk, eggs, zucchini, spices, vanilla, baking powder, baking soda and sweetener. Blend until smooth. Pour mixture into bowl and stir in bran. DO NOT ADD BRAN TO INGREDIENTS WHEN THEY ARE IN BLENDER BUT ONLY AFTER THEY HAVE BEEN POURED INTO THE BOWL. Pour into prepared pan and bake at 350 degrees for approximately 30 minutes. Cool in pan.

VARIATIONS:

1. In place of grated zucchini you may add 2 cored and grated apples, a 1-pound can of pumpkin (you may have to add up to ½ cup more of bran to absorb the extra amount of pumpkin) or 1 cup grated carrots.

2. As an additional treat, you may add 2 tablespoons raisins or raisins and unsalted nuts combined.

A Bit of Everything

Low-Calorie Carrot Cake

Preheat oven to: 350 degrees
Utensils needed: 2 mixing bowls; bundt pan,
greased and floured
Baking time: 1 hour

2 cups grated carrots
1 cup cored and
  grated Granny
  Smith apples
½ cup chopped fresh
  pineapple
1 cup currants
1 tablespoon grated
  orange peel
1 cup frozen apple-
  juice concentrate
1 tablespoon pure
  vanilla extract
2½ cups pastry flour
2 cups whole-wheat
  pastry flour

1 tablespoon baking
  powder
1 teaspoon baking
  soda
1½ tablespoons
  ground cinnamon
1 teaspoon pumpkin-
  pie spice
¼ cup nonfat yogurt
½ cup low-fat or
  skimmed
  buttermilk
3 stiffly beaten egg
  whites

Combine carrots, fruit, orange peel, apple-juice concentrate and vanilla in a mixing bowl. Stir to blend. Cover and refrigerate at least 12 hours.

Sift together all dry ingredients in a large mixing bowl. Make a well in center and stir in marinated carrot-fruit mixture. Add yogurt and buttermilk and stir until well combined.

Fold in beaten egg whites.

Pour into prepared pan and bake at 350 degrees for 1 hour or until edges pull away from pan.

Remove from pan and cool on wire rack.

Eggless Chocolate Cake

Preheat oven to: 350 degrees
Utensils needed: Mixing bowl; 8-inch-square
pan, greased and floured
Baking time: 30 minutes

1 cup water
1 tablespoon pure
  vanilla extract
5 tablespoons
  safflower oil
2 teaspoons white
  vinegar
1 teaspoon fresh
  lemon juice

1½ cups all-purpose
  flour
1 cup sugar
¼ cup cocoa powder
1 teaspoon baking
  soda
1½ teaspoon baking
  powder

Blend the water, vanilla, oil, vinegar and lemon juice. Set aside.

Sift all dry ingredients together in a mixing bowl. Stir in the liquid and beat until smooth. Batter should be runny.

Pour into prepared pan and bake for 30 minutes or until a toothpick inserted in the center comes out clean.

Remove from pan and cool on wire rack.

NOTE: This cake may be served plain, sprinkled with confectioner's sugar or iced with your favorite frosting.

Flourless Chocolate Cake

Preheat oven to: 350 degrees
Utensils needed: Double boiler; Electric mixer; 13 x 9 x 2-inch baking pan, greased with nonstick cooking spray
Cooking time: 45 minutes

1½ cups superfine sugar	¼ cup light-brown sugar
14 ounces semisweet chocolate	2 teaspoons pure vanilla extract
2 ounces unsweetened chocolate	10 large egg yolks
3 tablespoons hot water	10 large egg whites
	confectioner's sugar

Combine sugars, chocolates, hot water and vanilla extract in top half of double boiler over simmering water. Stir until chocolate is melted and mixture is very smooth. Remove from heat.

Beat yolks and gradually whisk into chocolate until well blended.

Beat egg whites until stiff. Stir ¼ of the beaten egg whites into chocolate to lighten mixture. Fold in remaining egg whites.

Pour into prepared pan and bake at 350 degrees for about 45 minutes or until cake pulls away from sides of pan. Remove from pan and cool on wire rack.

Packing for Shipping

No matter how tasty your homemade gift, if you pack it so poorly that it reaches its destination broken or spilled, no one will ever know what a good cook you are.

Breads and cakes should be wrapped in foil or plastic wrap, labeled and gift-wrapped. With the exception of fruit-cakes, these should not be shipped long distances unless they are air-mailed on the day of baking. Wrap the gift-wrapped parcel in a thick layer of newspaper, place in a heavy box at least 1 inch larger all around, pack tightly with shredded paper and wrap with heavy brown paper. Mark PERISHABLE and HANDLE WITH CARE.

Some cookies are better shippers than others. Bar and drop cookies are among the best. We find that cookies arrive in better shape when they are wrapped individually and packed in the box in layers separated by crumpled tissue. Wrap the box in the same manner described for breads and cakes. Place the gift parcel in a heavy cardboard box at least 3 inches larger all around and proceed as above.

As mentioned in the candy chapter, we do not suggest sending candies long distances. If you do wish to try shipping candy, wrap each piece individually and proceed as for cookies.

Nuts are good shippers. Pack them in a can and place it in a box at least 1 inch larger all around. Pack the box tightly with crumbled newspaper.

All homemade gifts that are in bottles or jars must be packed very carefully for shipping. If you are shipping more than one jar in a box, be sure you allow ample room around each—at least 3 inches. Wrap each jar in a heavy layer of newspaper. Before putting jars in shipping container, cover the bottom with a heavy layer of newspaper or shredded foam. (We highly recommend foam, as it will absorb more shock if the parcel is thrown about during shipment.) Place the wrapped jars in the box, well-separated, and pack more shredded paper or foam as tightly as possible around them. Pack the top of the box just as you did the bottom, finishing with a thick layer of newspaper. Label as for others and add FRAGILE.

When shipping many different goodies in one large box, always wrap each in plastic or foil. If one thing breaks or spills, this protects others from absorbing the liquid or odors.

INDEX

**Photography Credits For
Silhouetted Photographs**
© Christopher Bain: 40
© AGE Fotostock/FPG International:109
© Floyd Jillson/FPG International: 51
© Brian Leatart: 62b, 82
© Robert Lima/Envision: 116
© Bill Margerin/FPG International: 61b
© Charles Schneider/FPG
  International: 132
© J. Trefethen/FPG International: 68b, 130